THE THREE C1

'I have tried to define and
express what it means to me,
a potential musician, nurtured
in countryside of companionable
hills, two lovely but diverse rivers
amd three magnificent cathedrals.
It seems that Severn and Wye
flow through one's veins…
and the astonishing Three Choirs
Festivals go their historic way.'

Herbert Howells

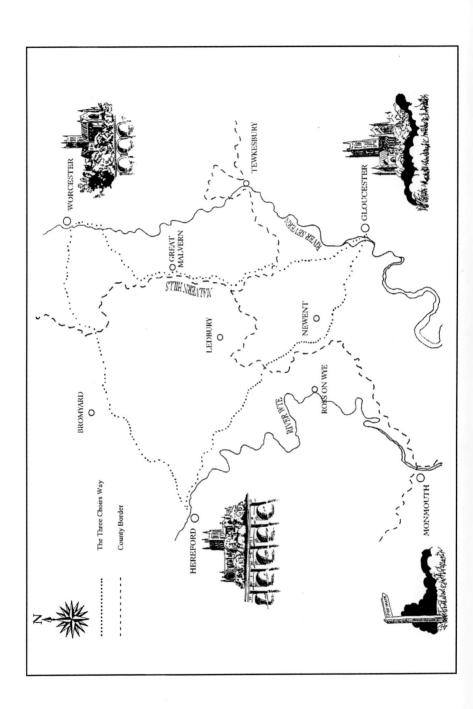

N

The Three Choirs Way ....

County Border - - - - - -

WORCESTER

TEWKESBURY

GREAT
MALVERN

MALVERN HILLS

LEDBURY

NEWENT

RIVER SEVERN

GLOUCESTER

BROMYARD

RIVER WYE

ROSS ON WYE

HEREFORD

MONMOUTH

The Three Choirs Way

GLOUCESTER – HEREFORD – WORCESTER

Only the wanderer
  Knows England's graces,
Or can anew see clear
  Familiar faces

And who loves joy as he
  That dwells in shadows?
Do not forget me quite
  O Severn meadows.

Ivor Gurney

Designed and compiled by
Gerry Stewart

COUNTRYSIDE MATTERS

First published in 1999
This revised and reset edition published in 2023 by
COUNTRYSIDE MATTERS
15 Orchard Road
Alderton
Tewkesbury
Gloucestershire GL20 8NS

Origination by Ex Libris Press
St Helier, Jersey

Printed by TPM (UK) Limited
Farrington Gurney, Somerset

© 2023 Gerry Stewart

ISBN 97809527870 6 8

Contents

Introduction

The origins of the Three Choirs Festivals were very informal beginning as friendly gatherings of the individual music clubs in each city. In 1879 'The Worcester Postman' reported that "the yearly musical assembly of these parts, held last year in Gloucester, will meet at Worcester on the last day of August". As centres of musical interest it was natural that they would sometimes combine choral services but, in 1720, Dr Thomas Bisse, Chancellor of Hereford Cathedral, proposed that future meetings should be for the benefit of widows and orphans of clergy. As a result from 1724 the Festivals became more formally organised events.

Although popular throughout Britain and Europe, some festivals, such as Bath and Cheltenham are of comparatively recent origin while others have faded from memory. The continuity of the Three Choirs Festival is unique, since they began before the births of Haydn, Mozart and Beethoven and only shortly after the deaths of Handel and Bach. It is the oldest musical festival in Europe and the list of composers such as Elgar, Holst, Vaughan Williams, Berkeley, Walton, Bliss, Britten and Finzi, is impressive.

An anecdote that accords pleasantly in a walking book, is of Gustav Holst arriving at Gloucester cathedral to conduct a choral rehearsal, soaking wet from the knees down having walked 'an ancient Roman trackway' to reach the cathedral. No doubt walkers of the Three Choirs Way will have occasion to commiserate.

*   *   *

The Three Choirs Way is mainly on footpaths and bridleways although few permissive paths are also used where they are preferable to the right of way, for instance along the bank of the

6

INTRODUCTION

Lugg at Mordiford.

The sketch maps with the text are quite adequate but to relate to the surrounding countryside Explorer maps are ideal.

Changes continually take place in the countryside, hedges still disappear and new fences arise, sometimes without stiles or gates, and crops may disguise the route. Recent path changes may not be reflected in current maps and although the highway authority's signposting should reveal these the situation may not always be clear on the ground.

Public transport links the three cities but it is difficult to co-ordinate elsewhere in the countryside. Hired transport is an economic way of getting to the start or finish of a days walk.

Climate change seems to have increased the incidence of flooding in many low lying areas and the rivers at Gloucester, Worcester and Hereford can severely affect the local footpaths when the only option then may be wide detours.

Some walkers of the Three Choirs Way have mentioned that they would prefer to avoid the cities, suggesting that the cathedrals are best visited on more leisurely occasions. For some apparently pastoral views of the cathedrals are more satisfying.

For them alternative routes avoiding the city centres are described at the approaches to Hereford and Worcester, while at Gloucester little urban walking is necessary.

Care has been taken to ensure that the information provided is accurate but neither author nor publisher can accept responsibility for any errors or omissions and particularly for the interpretation of the information by users.

Acknowledgments

This book arose from a series of walks combined with visits to Three Choirs Festival events inaugurated by Geoff and Joy Emms in 1987.

Geoff wrote of the first visit to Gloucester cathedral, "Inside, the evening sunlight flooded through the stained glass windows to provide a fitting backcloth for Elgar at his best. Even the bats joining in the performance".

It is in appreciation of the enthusiasm and innovative pleasures of country walking flavoured with music and poetry which they generated in their fellow walkers, that the Three Choirs Way is intended for them.

I also recall the kind help of many friends on the first exploratory walks and in particular, Margaret and Graham Davies, George Gilbody and Peter Collins who corrected a few flaws in my descriptions.

In rewriting most of this second edition of the Three Choirs Way my thanks are again due again to my daughter Genny Proctor for the new pen drawings, to Margaret Davies for route checking and to Kate for her support and again tackling the proof reading.

*   *   *

My thanks are also due for the kind permissions to use the poetry which enhances the enjoyment of the Three Choirs Way for many walkers: Trustees of the Gurney Estate: 'Song' from *The Collected Poems*'by Ivor Gurney; Alan Holden: 'Worcestershire Lanes' from *Selected Poems* 1987 by Molly Holden; Jeffrey Cooper: 'Ryton Firs' from *Twelve Idylls* by Lascelles Abercrombie; Robin Ivy: 'Severn' from *Worcestershire Suite*, 1992; Robert Wade: 'The Wye at Hereford' from *Verses;* Geoffrey Mason: 'Carpenters'.

May Hill

Gloucester to Clifford's Mesne

Until the building of the Severn bridges, Gloucester was, for centuries, the major crossing point of the Severn, an ancient frontier and centre for trade. The Romans early established a fort and Glevum became a place of retirement for officers and administrators. Wherever a hole is dug in the city it is said that 2000 years of occupation will be found.

Following the Romans and Saxons, the Normans commenced work on the cathedral, the tower, 225 feet high, is a landmark clearly seen for many miles.

In 1089 William the Conqueror ordered the preparation of Doomsday Book from his parliament in Gloucester.

Edward II, murdered at nearby Berkeley, was entombed in the cathedral which resulted in its becoming a place of pilgrimage. The prosperity which followed provided the 3000 inhabitants with a total of five monasteries and twelve churches, later giving rise to Shakespeare's comment "as sure as Gods' in Gloucester".

Unfortunately, the city elders backed Cromwell in the Civil War withstanding a determined and expensive siege by the Kings forces in 1643. On his restoration the King sought his due and caused the city walls, which would have been the equal of York's or Chester's today, to be demolished.

Modern road construction has obliterated much of the mediaeval causeway from Westgate out of the city, and a direct route to Telford's bridge no longer exists.

From the Cathedral walk down Westgate Street to reach the River Severn. A pedestrian flyover partly provides a safe crossing of the inner ring-road and a pedestrian bridge helps to avoid traffic crossing the eastern arm of the river. Then follow an underpass right and left to a footway past houses at Pool Meadow.

Walk away from the river for 100 yards to a gate and follow a track through parkland to a kissing gate commemorating the Millennium Heritage Grant for the Gloucestershire Way. Walk under a railway viaduct and turn left along a field edge to a kissing gate.

Pass beneath the pillars of the flyover and cross the water meadow to the grass ramp to Telford's Bridge spanning the west channel of the Severn. Now a English Heritage site the bridge together with Brunel's Great Western Railway alongside, is a pleasant historical interlude in the face of the nearby rush and roar of more modern traffic. The bridge also provides passage for both the Gloucestershire and Wysis Ways and a cycle/footway.

The Wysis Way is a long distance path linking two national trails, the Offa's Dyke Path at Monmouth and the Thames Path at Kemble.

The Gloucestershire Way runs for 100 miles from Chepstow Castle to Tewkesbury Abbey through the diverse areas of the Forest of Dean, Severn Vale and Cotswold.

Designed by Thomas Telford and copied from a bridge over the Seine it was opened in 1831. The arch is a graceful ellipse enhanced by the chamfering of the stonework to ease the flow of floodwaters. A keen eye will detect where the crown of the arch sank considerably when the scaffolding was first removed. No doubt a heart stopping moment for the masons and engineers, but Telford is said to have expected it! The bridge replaced a 13th century structure described by the historian Leland... a seven arch stone bridge nearest the city, then one of five arches, followed by 'the great causey of stone forced up through the low meads of Severne' and finally a bridge of eight arches.

Leaving the bridge site turn right to a cycle/footway passing under the carriageways and at the far side continue for about 350 yards passing the Dog Inn and at Over Farm shop turn in to Lassington Lane. After half a mile or so the lane bends left and a kissing gate gives access into Lassington Wood. A path along the bottom edge of the wood gradually rises to exit at a kissing gate. Immediately turn right over a stile and walk diagonally left to a further stile to the roadside at the dormitory suburb of Maidenhall.

Nearby is Highnam Court, where Thomas Gambier Parry was often host to notable composers including Elgar and Vaughan Williams. His son Hubert had his first success as a composer, with 'Prometheus Unbound', at the Gloucester Festival of 1880.

Hubert's lectures, on the history of music, later enthralled Holst and Vaughan Williams, but his major fame is for the music to Blake's immortal 'Jerusalem'.

From the stile walk down the wide grass verge close to the hedge and through trees descend a short slope to a stile into a narrow field. At the far end cross a stile and turn left along a track which joins a lane in to Lassington.

A mediaeval village site, the disused church, originally Saxon, was dedicated on Palm Sunday 1095 AD.

Turn left between the farm buildings and follow the bridleway across a field for about 250 yards before turning right across the open field. At the edge of the woodland follow an indistinct track left gradually descending through undergrowth to a bridle gate into a field.

Begun in 1792 and completed in 1845, the Herefordshire and Gloucestershire canal was virtually forgotten until recent years.
From the Severn at Gloucester via Newent, Dymock and Ledbury the canal was 34 miles in length with 22 locks and three tunnels.
The canal closed in 1881 to allow the construction of the Gloucester to Newent railway with the track being over much of the canal bed. The Three Choirs Way meets the canal again at Withington near Hereford.

From the gate follow the shallow depression of the old canal curving right across the low lying field and as the bridleway bears left to the road continue, now on a footpath through a gate on the right. Turn left to a stile and follow the line of both railway and canal alongside the hedge.

After about 300 yards turn left over a stile. *This was the site of a lock basin on the canal and a footbridge crossed from the stile to the lockkeepers house and the tow path.*

Over the stile continue following the hedge to a lane close to Rudford church. Cross through the kissing gate opposite and descend the embankment to regain the track bed and follow it to the Newent – Gloucester road. Cross to a path up the embankment carrying the old road over the bridge which once spanned the railway and from the parapet look down on the buildings of Barbers Bridge Station.

During the excavations for the earlier canal almost a hundred skeletons were found in a communal grave nearby. They are thought to have been soldiers of the Welsh army supporting King Charles during his siege of Gloucester but who were overwhelmed in retreat when Roundhead forces relieved the city.

The bloody skirmish at the nearby stream crossing is commemorated in both 'Barberous Bridge' and the 'Red Brook' and further by the road side obelisk built out of stone from the demolished city walls.

Resuming from the bridge turn right along a field edge path to Bovone Farm. The path continues between farm buildings and then diagonally left down a sloping field and through a gate at the bottom.

Walk left, around the hedge corner and cross the field to a footbridge. Continue behind houses to a road and turn right downhill to a junction. Turn right and then left, passing the village duck pond, and walk up to a footpath on the right just prior to Tibberton church.

The track descends, *with May Hill and Ragged Stone Hill at the end of the Malvern ridge prominent,* to open fields and a junction of paths. Fork left across a field to a stile, then inclining left, walk a long field to double stiles and continue to a footbridge into parkland. Again incline left, leaving oak trees to the right and cross a farm drive to a stile in the hedge ahead, just to the right of a concrete farm road.

From the stile, Wysis Way continues towards May Hill, instead fork right, over the shoulder of the slight ridge where the path follows a line towards two tall conifers on the horizon and down to a gate where two paths diverge, follow that to the left up to Taynton church, a pleasant spot to pause.

Leaving the church entrance cross the road to a kissing gate and walk down the field to join the farm track to Drew's Farm. Cross a stream and after passing the house and last of the farm outbuildings, former pig sties, turn left through a gate and walk along the field edge to a stile.

Cross the next field and through a gate walk slightly right up to a gate into the farm yard at The Hill. The gateway can be extremely muddy but if too difficult can be avoided over the low wire fence on left and crossing grass to a hand gate. Through the yard incline right and where the farm drive bends left continue right into the remains of a green lane.

Emerging into open field, the old way can be traced along the boundary hedge to the next corner. Now change direction by climbing the stile and bank on the right, at Cole's Barn.

Walk directly down the large field cross the farm bridge and climb the slope keeping about 50 yards from the tree belt which surrounds Ploddy House on the right. Over the brow walk straight down to join the Taynton - Newent road and turn right at Little Cugley.

Round a bend and turn left on a footpath beneath an oak tree and angle right over the low ridge and down to a stile. From this walk left converging with the hedge at a gate and through this follow the hedge up hill to a stile in the cross hedge.

Cross this and a second on the left walk over the slight rise in the ground and then down to a further stile and steps down the steep hedge bank.

Cross the sloping field midway between the dominating pylons and power lines but from the last pylon descend the slope bearing left to an often boggy area and a kissing gate under the trees.

Angle left up the slope of an earth dam and at the top follow the edge of the ponds to the right and continue to exit through another kissing gate. Follow the track to a road junction at Woodgate.

Walk straight on for half a mile along the edge of Newent Wood and passing an old perry orchard over the hedge to the right. *Cider was once a common drink in rural areas, every farm had a cider orchard and most cottages at least one apple or pear tree. Perry, as its name suggests, was made solely from pears.*

From the next junction, where the Yew Tree Inn is a quarter of a mile left, follow the road bending right to a narrow cross road and continue uphill past houses until the road becomes a track. After the last dwelling climb a stile on the right and walk up the field aiming right of a red roofed cottage, to a gate on to a lane. *Lean on the gate and look back, trying to ignore the forest of pylons, over the wide panorama of the vale. In reasonable weather Gloucester cathedral will be clear in the distance.*

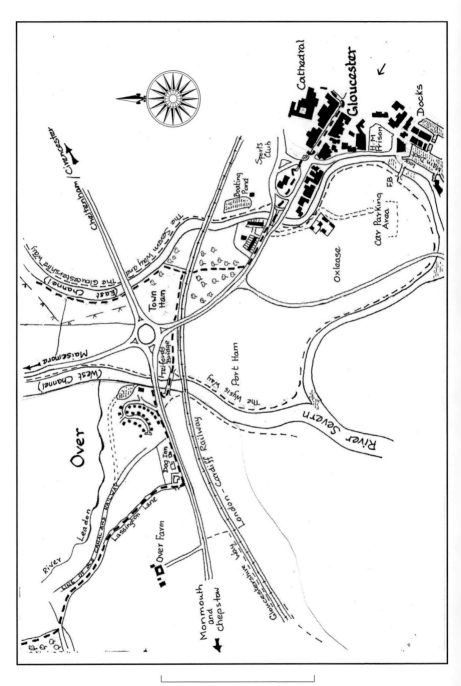

Half mile

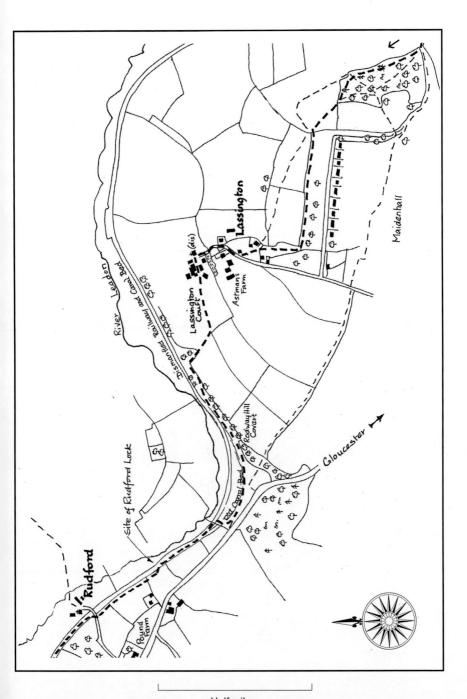

Lassington

Maidenhall

River Leadon

Disminantled Railway and Canal Bed

(dis)

Lassington Court

Astmani Farm

Rodway Hill Covart

Old Canal Bed

Gloucester

Site of Rudford Lock

Rudford

Round Farm

Half mile

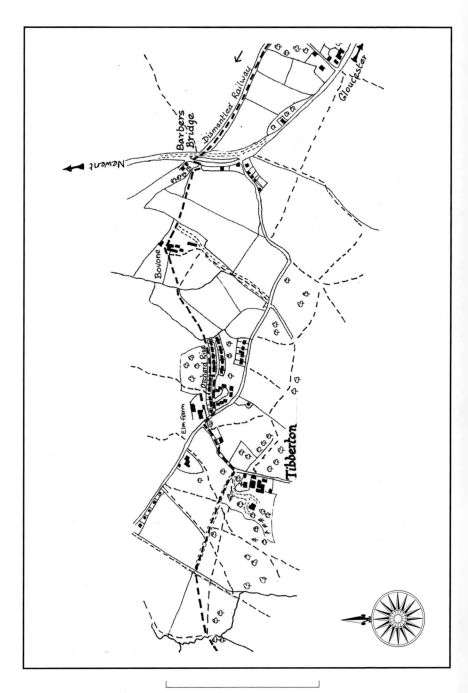

Half mile

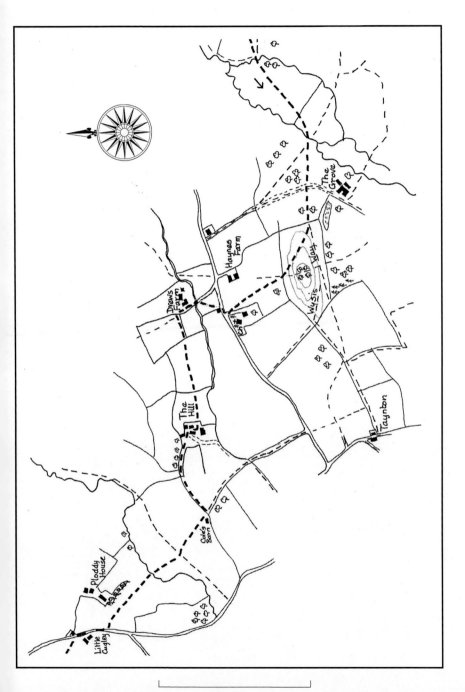

Half mile

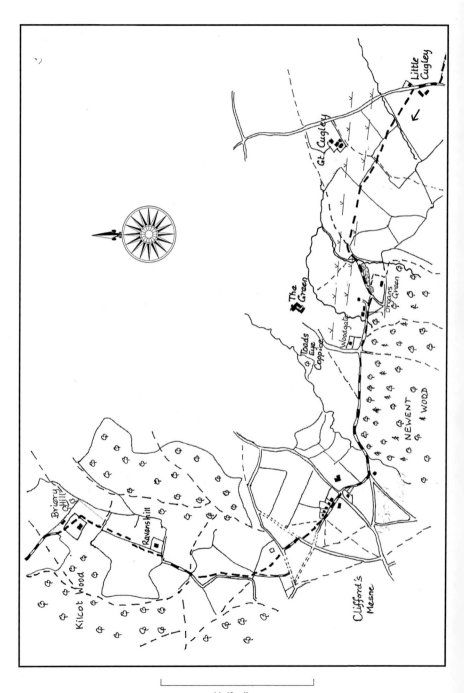

Half mile

Newent
Colliery
(site of)

Clifford's Mesne to Sleaves Oak

From the gate walk up the lane to a junction go through a kissing gate in front. Walk past a horse ménage and negotiate electric fences to converge with the hedge on the right at a kissing gate. *The view, without pylons, is now west and north to May Hill and the Marcle ridge dominated by its tall mast. In the distance beyond the line of the Malverns are the Suckley hills.*

Walk down the field inclining towards the hedge on the left and where this bends away continue down to a kissing gate in the bottom corner. Follow the track beyond curving right to an isolated house, Ravenshill.

Just before reaching the house go through a gate on the left and walk down the field edge for about 150 yards and change to the other side of the hedge through a kissing gate. Continue, again with extensive views from this slight ridge, to a kissing gate at the field bottom.

Cross the slight slope in front and walk down close to the boundary of another house, Briery Hill and go through a field gate into the property. Walk the few yards down the driveway and exit through a second gate and continue down the access track with Kilcot Wood to the left.

The track eventually levels and past a house on the left fork left through woodland to reach the Newent - Ross road at Kilcot. Cross the road with care and continue down the narrow lane opposite.

At a junction turn right, passing a farmhouse and large barn, to a footpath on the left. Walk down the field edge to a gate on to Kews Lane and cross a few paces right to another gate and continue down to a rudimentary stile in the corner.

Continue diagonally down through an old cider orchard, past a hedge corner, to a bend in the Ell Brook and climb a stile in the corner to a track leading to Hill House Farm.

Turn left, crossing the brook, and after 50 yards go right though a gate.

The promise of reward arising from a coal field in this vicinity enthused the share holders of the Hereford-Gloucester Canal company to provide more funds for the project and resulted in a mile long branch from the line of the canal at Oxenhall to the nearby Hill House Colliery.

Cross the field at the bottom of the steep slope and after the remains of an old field boundary follow the hedge on the left for about 100 yards, where it bends sharply left walk across the low lying meadow to a hunt gate on an embankment opposite. *This is part of a culvert built in 1790 to carry the canal branch over the*

Brockmorehead Brook.

Through the gate keep left, following a lesser stream up a narrow valley to a gate on to a lane. *The steep hillock to the right is the remains of the spoil heap at the site of Newent Colliery.*

Turn left and after about 200 yards, join a footpath through a gate on the right. Walk up the field to a stile and over this continue up alongside the hedge.

At the top of the field, cross two stiles in succession and then branch right to a third in an angle of the hedge and walk up the next field towards a house and follow the garden boundary to a gate on to a road.

Turn right along the road for 100 yards and then left into the Forestry Commission's Greenaway's Wood . *(The Gloucestershire Nature Trust maintain the inviting meadowland sites at either side of the access gate.)*

Follow the main track through the wood ignoring other tracks left and right and descend slightly to a footbridge. Continue up the next field alongside the hedge to the boundary of Betty Daw's Wood also in the care of the Forestry Commission.

A kissing gate gives access to the wood but the Three Choirs Way follows a path left along the edge of the woodland. At the road turn left and then right and cross the noise and rush of traffic on the M50 motorway.

We have become complacent of this noise blight but along quiet footpaths through the woodland landscape of the Dymock Poets, it seems a great pity.

... when the green
Flashes with daffodils, From Marcle way,
From Dymock, Kempley, Newent, Bromsberrow,
Redmarley, all the meadowland daffodils seem
Running in golden tides to Ryton Firs,
To make the knot of steep little wooded hills
Their brightest show. . .

Lascelles Abercrombie

In the years leading up to the First World War, literary history was being made in the valley of the Leadon around Dymock. Although the 'muse colony' as they came to be known; Lascelles Abercrombie, Wilfred Gibson and Robert Frost; were not Gloucestershire poets, they received many visitors during their stay who were also destined to become well known. Of these, Rupert Brooke, perhaps the most well known, and Edward Thomas, were shortly to die in war. Among local poets who visited the colony, John Drinkwater and WH Davies later lived in the county. John Haines, a Gloucester solicitor, was a regular visitor and particular friend of Robert Frost. Haines encouraged Ivor Gurney, a fellow choral scholar of Herbert Howells, and FW (Will) Harvey who were to become acknowledged poets of Gloucestershire.

From the motorway continue for about 250 yards to a footpath on the left following a forestry track into Dymock Wood. *Sessile oak is prominent and is typical of the areas bordering Wales. Acorns are collected by Forest Enterprise and stored at a nursery at Delamere in Cheshire for wider distribution.*

As part of the local Daffodil Way away from the forest track the path has been gravelled and is well waymarked.

The Daffodil Way is a circular walk of two miles through countryside renowned for its wild daffodils which once provided seasonal work for itinerant labour, the city markets being supplied by rail. Although much diminished, the woods and hedgerows are still thick with wild varieties in the spring.

The path eventually emerges from the wood through a kissing gate into the remains of a cider orchard.

Cross a brook near a willow tree and walk up to the left of extensive farm buildings and follow the line of an old track bounded on the left by a row of cider perry trees and on the right by the distant Malvern ridge. Walk past the barns to a kissing gate in the corner and continue up the next field edge to a further kissing gate and pass between garden hedges to join the road into Kempley Green.

Pass a chapel of 1856 and then a gate where the Daffodil Way departs left and continue for another 200 yards before forking right into a green lane – not to be confused with a footpath to the right.

Follow the green lane, crossing a farm track, through a gate and then along a field edge. *In the middle distance is the church tower of Much Marcle with the Marcle ridge and ubiquitous mast, further left.* Just before reaching the next boundary go through a gate on the left and turn right down the field edge.

Kempley has two churches. St Edward's, built in 1903 of local stone from the Forest of Dean, and described by John Betjeman as 'a miniature cathedral of the Arts and Crafts movement', can be visited by a footpath to the left climbing up the field.

Continue alongside the hedge, slightly uphill and curving right, to a gate onto a lane. Turn left and walk down for a 100 yards, to a footpath on the right under a large oak tree. Follow the hedge of this long field, with a stream on the other side, to a gate just before Kempley Court. Bear right with the stream and pass a footbridge to another gate, through this cross a horse paddock and continue through further gates and close to farm buildings, towards the squat tower of the older church.

Cross a footbridge and then a large stone slab over tributaries of the Kempley Brook, to St Mary's church. *The church contains extensive frescoes, some as fresh as when painted in 1130 – older than many of the important church paintings of Florence and Rome. The building is now managed by English Heritage.*

At the road turn left and cross to a gate where two footpaths diverge. Fork right across the corner of the field to a stile. *Although the path followed is a fairly direct line the ancient field boundaries around Friar's Court dictate a convoluted description.*

Follow the ditch line left for a short distance and then angle right to a stile in the next boundary. Bear right to converge with the next hedgerow and after about 100 yards cross a stile and plank bridge in the field corner.

Turn left to a further stile and footbridge then cross a narrow field below Friar's Court. Cross the next long field to a stile and a narrow field to a footbridge in a thick hedge, *the boundary between Gloucestershire into Herefordshire.* Cross two further fields to reach the road from Dymock and follow it left into Much Marcle - which has a village shop and three pubs. *Mear- cleah, old English - a boundary wood.*

Enter the churchyard under the yew arch and pass an ancient

cross to the famed and impressive Marcle Yew. *Thought to be at least 1,500 years old, stand beside it and consider the history which the tree stood silent witness to since Roman times.*

Unlettered carpenters,
After four hundred years
Nothing is left of them,
Even their bones are dust.

They put the axe to oak,
The saw, adze and chisel;
Unlettered carpenters
Nothing is left of them

Whose eyes grew narrower
From saw-pit to grave-pit;
After four hundred years
Even their bones are dust.
Unlettered carpenters,
After four hundred years,
All that is left of them -
V V O O X X
(Carpenters marks to assist assembly of structure)
Geoffrey Mason

Leave the churchyard under another yew arch and cross a track to a stile. Descend the field diagonally right to a gate in the corner. Cross a road and angle slightly left across the field to a footbridge.

Continue on the same line up to a gap follow the hedge up a long field to a minor road. Cross slightly left, and over a stile walk up the slope inclining right over the shoulder of the ridge to another minor road. Cross this into a track and follow it winding uphill past cottages at Marcle Hill.

There are splendid views from these slopes. Ledbury is clearly seen below the Malvern ridge and beyond Marcle Church, the Severn plain to the Cotswold scarp.

John Masefield was born at Ledbury in 1878,and the countryside around the Malvern Hills and Hereford influenced his works throughout his life. His vigorous narrative poems, like 'The Everlasting Mercy', and 'Reynard the Fox' are colourful descriptions of the local countryside. For a time he and Elgar were pre-eminent he as Poet Laureate and Elgar as Master of the King's Music.

Cross a stile at Marcle Hill and turn left to a further stile then right following the hedge to join a track at Little Puckmore. Walk up to join a lane and turn uphill for 300 yards to a sharp bend.

Leave the lane and continue uphill on a rough track. As this starts to descend sharply *the extensive view is now west over the ridges and woods of the Forest of Dean and the far flung hills of Wales.* Turn right climbing a stile and steps leading to the Marcle ridge.

Climb the slope for a few yards and through a gate on the left follow an enclosed green track for three quarters of a mile, passing the lofty mast and a Trig pillar.

In the east all the outlying hills of Cotswold can be identified, and in the south May Hill seems close at hand. Under a westering sun Gloucester Cathedral stands clear in the vale.

The track ends at a stile but over this continue left along the field edge for a further half mile before descending steep steps to a narrow road at Sleaves Oak.

* * *

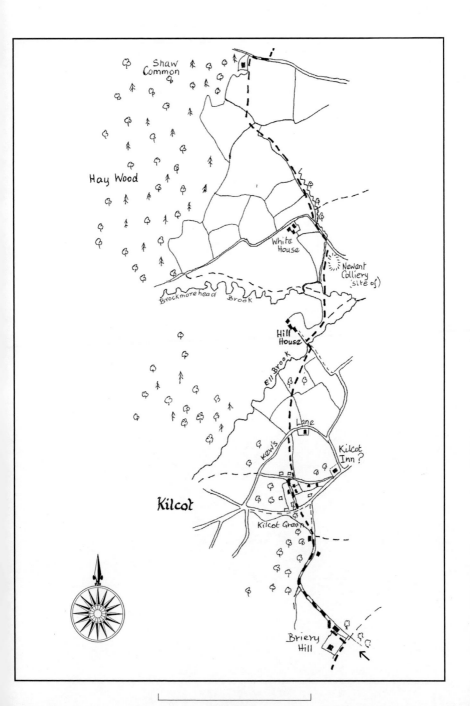

Half mile

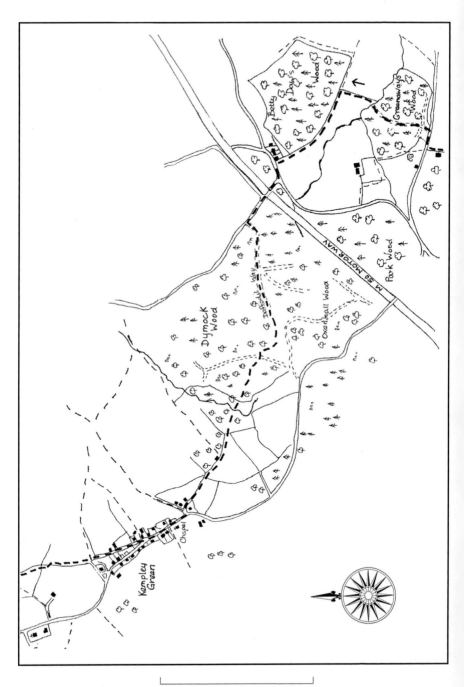

Half mile

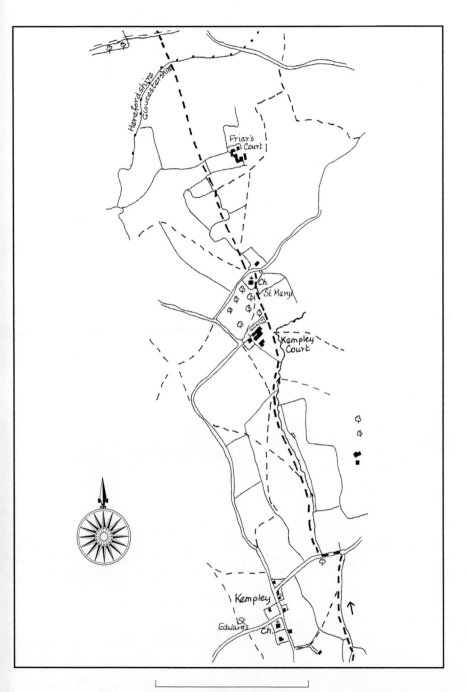

Hereford shire
Gloucestershire

Friar's Court

Ch.
St Marys

Kempley
Court

Kempley
St
Edward's Ch.

Half mile

Reproduced by kind permission of Ordnance Survey © Crown Copyright MC/99-073

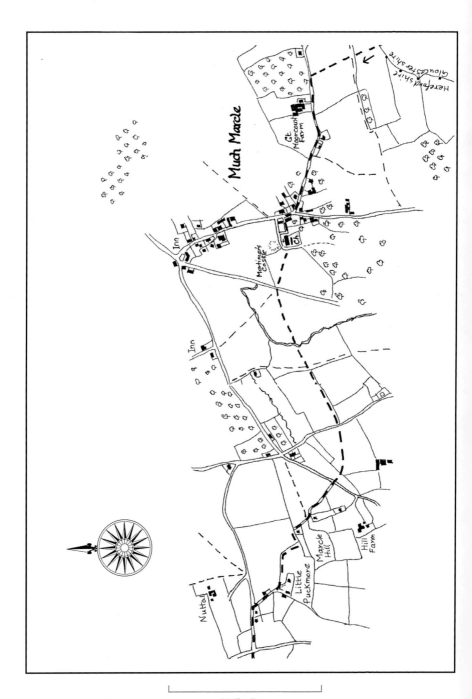

Much Macle

Gt. Moorcourt Farm

Herefordshire
Gloucestershire

Inn

Morlmer's Castle

Ch

Inn

Marcle Hill

Hill Farm

Little Puckmore

Nutta

Half mile

Reproduced by kind permission of Ordnance Survey © Crown Copyright MC/99-073

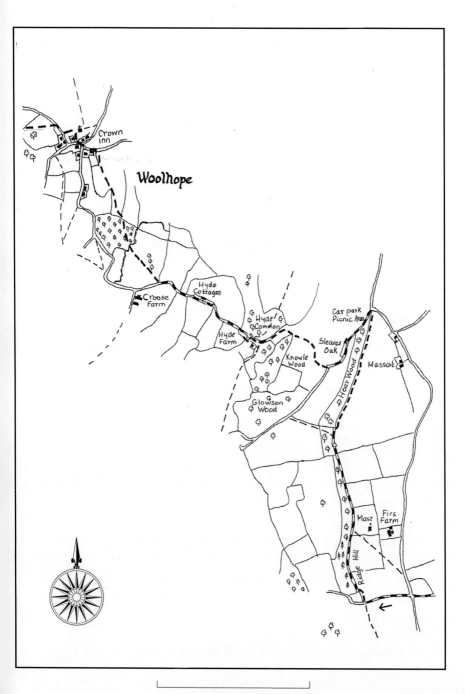

Woolhope

Crown Inn

Croose Farm

Hyde Cottages

Hyde Common

Hyde Farm

Knowle Wood

Glowson Wood

Car park Picnic Area

Sleaves Oak

Hoar Wood

Messcot

Mast

Firs Farm

Ridge Hill

Half mile

The Marcle Yew – possibly 2,000 years old

Sleaves Oak to Hereford Cathedral

Walk down the narrow lane to the left for a quarter of a mile, passing a house Sleaves Oak, and bending right and then sharply left. Turn right at a gate under an oak tree and walk down the slope to a barn at the bottom and turn left along a track to Hyde Farm. Follow the track right between farm buildings, where it shortly becomes a public road.

In less than half a mile after a left bend with the road beginning to descend, cross a stile on the right and walk down the field passing a small copse of horse chestnut, oak and lime trees. Cross a footbridge and walk diagonally right through an apple orchard to a stile and over this turn left to a further stile. Continue angling right up past a hedge corner with the squat tower of Woolhope Church showing, on a line to the right of houses and cross two more stiles to the road.

Commencing well before the Roman occupation Herefordshire

34

has a long history of cider making, where mild springs and warm summers promote tree growth and ripen the fruit.
Thomas Knight of Hereford, was the first systematic cultivator of new apple varieties. His 'Pomona Herefordiensis' of 1691, was the first illustrated book describing cider apples and pears. The original cider apple was small and bitter, but some 265 varieties evolved through the art of grafting and budding.
Cider orchards which once enhanced many farms have gone. Today's cider is, in the main, commercially produced from limited varieties to maintain a standard product far removed from that of traditional cider apples.

'Coccagee and Bloody Butcher:
Slack- ma-Girdle,
Red Soldier and Lady's Finger,
Kingston Black, Bloody Turk,
Foxwhelp, Pawson, Tom Putt,
Bitter Sweet and Fatty Mutt.'

Turn left and walk up to the Crown Inn and possibly refreshment, otherwise follow an old paved path through the adjoining churchyard beneath a pair of splendid Lime trees.

Although a long way from Coventry a window in the church features Lady Godiva - properly Godgifu. She and her sister Wuliva are connected with Woolhope where they once owned the manor. Woolhope may be contracted from 'Wuliva's Hope' - Hope being an enclosed valley or hollow.

The 'Woolhope Dome' is a local area of geological interest containing rocks, fossils and a particular limestone. It spawned a Naturalists Field Club in 1854 and an early president was Alfred Watkins of Hereford who propounded the theory of ancient Ley Lines in the countryside and was author of 'The

Old straight Track'.

Pass the church to a gate and walk through the parking area to the road. Turn right and cross to a kissing gate into a field. Pass close to an oak tree and then follow the edge of the woodland to the right. Continue through a second kissing gate and, after 50 yards, a third, into the woodland. Follow a stream uphill to a crossing place where the stream has been dammed and turn right, through pleasant meadow land. *Marked as 'The Leys' on the OS map – meaning medieval pasture or fallow land.*

After a final kissing gate, walk up hill to a gate onto a road and turn right, soon passing alongside part of Broadmoor Common. Continue past a road junction and houses at Haugh Wood Gate.

After a cream coloured house turn right onto a bridleway track but in a few yards, at a vehicle barrier, branch left and at a fork keep right on a path rising steadily through Haugh Wood, - *old English, haga - an enclosure, in this case of trees. 'A man- eating dragon once resided here, using a path, still called Serpent's Lane, down to Mordiford to terrorise the locality'.*

At a further fork as the path levels bear right and shortly descend over a cross path before climbing again to a junction with a major forestry road. Continue straight over the crest, ignoring a lesser track branching right, and descend to cross another forestry road.

At the next cross track go slightly left where the original hollow way, although sometimes narrow and overgrown, can be found. *Throughout Europe, new forestry tracks, particularly in hill areas, are created with little sympathy for the original paths and tracks often of great antiquity.*

Walk down this old route beneath a grove of cedars and emerge at a fence around a timber yard and follow this to the right to a stile. Over this join a track, passing a house, and continue pleasantly down for a quarter of a mile, to the road between Woolhope and Mordiford.

Turn right for about 300 yards, and then left on a bridleway which descends curving left, to Hope Springs. Nearing the buildings turn right into an enclosed lane, *shared with the Wye Valley Walk*, up past houses at Bagpiper's Tump.

The Wye Valley Walk commences at Chepstow Castle and follows, for 70 miles, the beautiful Wye Valley to Tintern, and then the meandering river past Monmouth, Ross-on Wye and Hereford, to Hay-on-Wye, deep in the Welsh Marches.

The bridleway continues between the buildings but with the Wye Valley Walk follow a footpath forking down to the right which becomes a pleasant green route. Through a gate walk down through an orchard following the hedge on the left. Cross a stream and follow it down crossing again at a farm bridge. Keep right of farm buildings to a gate into the farm yard and walk down to a road and either cross to a back lane leading to Mordiford Bridge and Church or turn right to the Moon Inn and village shop/post office. *Mordiford - Welsh, mawr-ty - a great house.*

The village grew around an ancient ford over the River Lugg. The original bridge dates from the 14th Century but was enlarged in the 16th. Two arches take the normal flow but all nine are necessary in time of flood.
The church records an occurrence 'on Monday, 27th May, 1811, between the hours of 5 and 9pm the village of Mordiford was

visited by a terrible storm, thunder, lightning, winds and rain, by which the little river of Pentaloe was swollen in places to extent of 180 feet and depth of 20 feet'. . . Four villagers were drowned.

Cross the bridge and flood arches, and turn right onto the floodbank (the Stank), also used by the Wye Valley Walk, and follow it alongside the Lugg for more than a mile. Close to Hampton Bishop continue through several gates, some with stiles alongside, to a lane leading to Court Farm. Turn left pass a right fork and at the next junction turn right.

Shortly after a double bend turn right on a footpath which follows the edge of a field and continues across to a stile onto a lay-by alongside the Mordiford to Hereford road. The 'Bunch of Carrots' Inn is 100 yards left.

Cross to the wider verge and climb steps to a path along the flood bank and follow it right through a kissing gate. After 40 yards or so leave the flood bank and from a footbridge cross the field to the bank of the River Wye.

Elgar was a violinist with both the Choral and Philhar-monic Societies at Hereford and he must have taken part in many Musical Festivals. Later, while living at Great Malvern, he was a regular visitor to Dr George Robertson Sinclair organist at Hereford Cathedral where they enjoyed walks together particularly along the banks of the Wye. Dr Sinclair and his dog Dan are celebrated in the 'Enigma Variations' arising from an incident when Dan slid down the steep bank into the river. Elgar's great love of the countryside and the Wye is reflected in his great choral music and parts of 'The Musicmakers' are said to have been composed at Mordiford Bridge.

Follow the riverside path through more kissing gates towards the spire of Tupsley Church showing above pink roofs ahead. Close to a large oak tree incline right to a final gate where a gravelled path between houses leads to the road.

Alternative Route to Lugwardine avoiding city and four miles of road walking

Turn right along the road for about 200 yards to a bridleway on the left, and follow Holywell Gutter Lane for almost a mile. At a road junction near Tupsley School turn right to reach the Ledbury Road at the 'Cock of Tupsley' where the main route joins from the left.

Otherwise continue towards Hereford and after about a mile pass under a railway bridge and immediately turn left into Outfall Works Road. Walk down this narrow road for about 400 yards, and just before crossing a small viaduct turn right down the embankment to a footpath crossing fields to Green Street.

The name invokes an image of the medieval approach to the city walls where the sight of the cathedral and castle probably gave great relief to travellers still fraught by tales of dragons in Haugh Wood and floodwaters at Mordiford.

Walk along Green Street for 50 yards and turn left into Vicarage Road. Past a school continue down a footpath to the river bank and turn right to the *Victoria* footbridge. Do not cross, but climb the steps to Castle Green *(the site of Hereford Castle)* and cross to the narrow streets around the cathedral.

> No common waters, by these ancient walls,
> Flow from Plynlimon's distant storm-filled springs,
> By many a changing mile the current brings
> By Ithon's vale and Ebbw's rock-bound falls

THE THREE CHOIRS WAY

And mountain moorlands where the curlew calls
A spell distilled of old and lovely things;
Cloud wrapped memorials of long dead Kings,
Forsaken castles and deserted halls.

The scattered dust of centuries lies blown
Along the valleys where the oaks are green,
Dressed by the summers of a thousand years
And all the sun and rain the years have known,
For all that is born of what has been;
From age to age its laughter and its tears.

Robert Wade

Hereford cider orchard

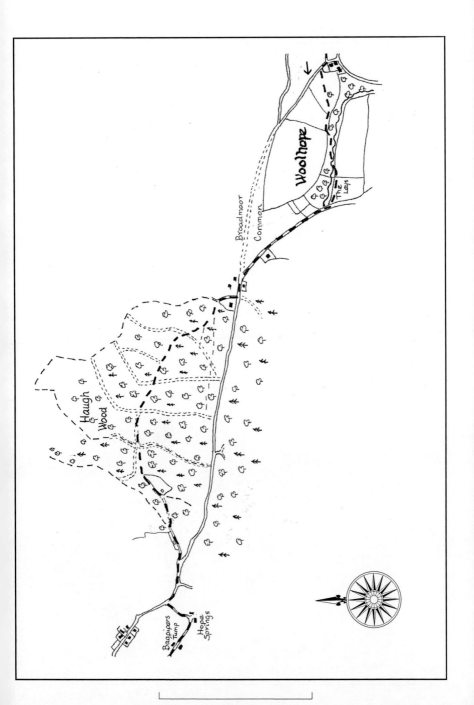

Half mile

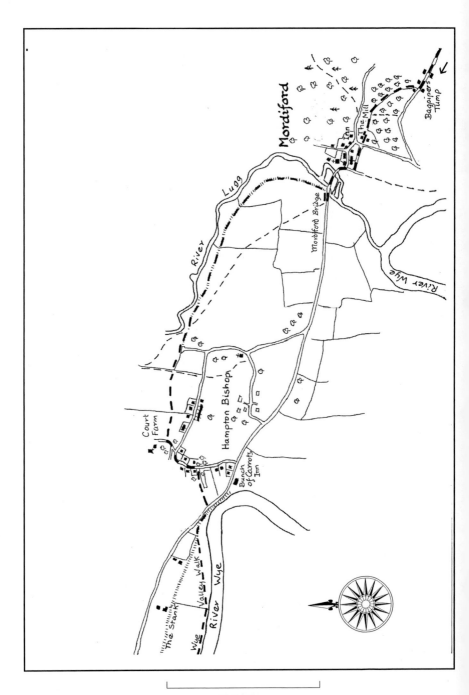

Half mile

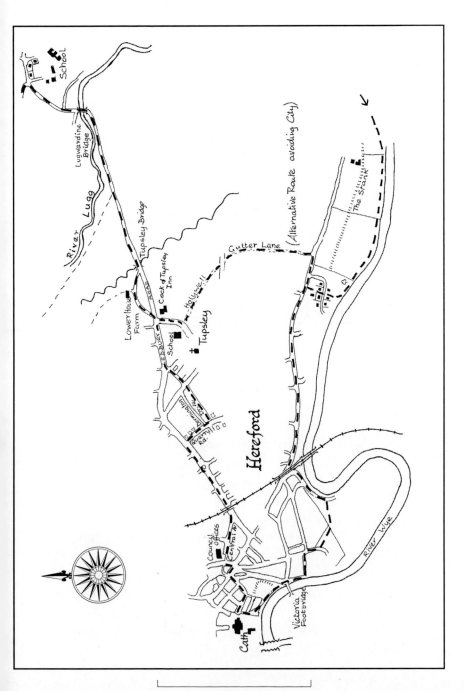

School

River Lugg

Lugwardine Bridge

Tupsley Bridge

Cock of Tupsley Inn

Lower House Farm

LEDBURY ROAD

Holywell

School

Tupsley

Cutter Lane

(Alternative Route avoiding City)

The Stank

Hereford

Quarry Rd.

Hampton Park Rd.

Council Offices

General Hospital

River Wye

Victoria Footbridge

Cath

Half mile

Hereford Cathedral

Hereford to Ocle Pychard

Anglo Saxon Charters refer to Here-paths, - literally meaning Army roads. Hereford may well have taken its name from a ford across the Wye 'the army ford' where Roman armies crossed in safety and the only method until a wooden bridge was built in the 12th Century. When that was destroyed by flood waters Richard II provided materials for repairs and granted toll rights for twenty years. The present Wye Bridge was built in 1490.

Established as a cathedral city in 676 AD, a stone cathedral existing before the Conquest was destroyed by Welsh invaders in 1055. The present building was begun by the Normans soon after their arrival.

The cathedral contains two unique treasures. The Mappa Mundi is a 13th Century map or 'estoire' - a history, on vellum. The coloured map, shows the world as a circle with Jerusalem at the centre and 'Britainnia Insula' almost off the edge, and contains a wealth of detail with the 'Wie' and 'Hford' marked.

The 'chained library', the largest in England, contains 1500 priceless books and manuscripts from as early as 1056 although the bookcases, with each volume chained to a horizontal bar, was introduced in 1611.
Hereford also boasts the second largest 'chained library', in All Saints Church.

David Garrick was born in Hereford in 1717 and Nell Gwynne, actress and favourite mistress of Charles II, is said to have been born here in 1651.

Sir Edward Elgar rose to become England's greatest composer for 200 years. In his early years he was a violinist with the Choral and Philharmonic Societies in Hereford and probably took part in many Musical Festivals. Later when becoming an established composer he was a regular visitor to Dr George Robertson Sinclair, the organist at Hereford. After receiving his knighthood in 1904 Elgar moved to Hereford where he composed some his best works, including the Violin Concerto and his two Symphonies. His great love of the countryside and of the Wye is reflected in his great choral music.

From the cathedral retrace your steps to Castle Street and continue into St Ethelbert Street. After passing Cantilope Street, turn right along St Owen's Street and after a short distance left into Bath Street. Cross the road to an enclosed path just left of Daw's Road and walk down this and then the length of Central Avenue using the left hand pavement, to join the Ledbury Road.

Continue past a roundabout for 300 yards and turn right into Quarry Road. Pass Dormington Drive on the left and then turn into a path beneath trees and shrubs adjacent to Tupsley Park. When this ends, turn right into Church Road and immediately left into Winchester Drive, merging into Salisbury Avenue and leads to Ledbury Road again.

Walk along the major road for about 350 yards and, opposite 'The Cock of Tupsley', (where the alternative route avoiding Hereford re-joins) turn left in to the old version of the Ledbury road and walk down passing Lower House Farm. *The headquarters of Herefordshire Nature Trust, the old farmhouse is well worth a visit.*

Rejoining the main road cross, first Tupsley Bridge followed by the causeway over the flood meadows and finally Lugwardine Bridge. *An iron plaque on the bridge informs passers that the cost of widening the bridge was met by 'local neighbourhood subscription and at the expense of the County'. A few yards further on pass a cast iron trough with working pump.*

After 400 yards turn left into Cott Road at Lugwardine, where the Crown and Anchor Inn may offer refreshment.

Lugwardine - settlement by the Lugg.
The water meadows cover several hundreds of acres and are part of a system of Tenure which has survived from pre-medieval times. Known as Lammas Lands, they are grazed 'in common', when the animals wander freely, from Lammas, 2nd August, to Candlemas, 2nd February. For the remainder of the year hay is grown 'in severalty', with individual strips separated from neighbouring strips by boundary stones. Problems and disputes are settled at an annual meeting at the Crown and Anchor Inn.

Past the pub follow the road bending right and after the last bungalow join a footpath on the right. Follow the field edge to a gap in the first boundary hedge and veer left to a stile in the next. Fork left from the stile to a hand gate then cross a stream and incline right under garden trees to join a stony track in front of a white thatched cottage. Follow this up to a road and turn right.

After 100 yards, with the road bending right, turn left on a narrow footpath sometimes concealed by shrubbery alongside a bungalow. Cross a stile and continue to a second stile alongside a gate and over this join a farm track and, after a kissing gate, follow it uphill. Where the track enters an open field continue across to the next boundary hedge but here turn left without crossing the stile.

From this slightly elevated position above the adjacent fields presents a wide panorama over north Herefordshire. The more spectacular view is behind. Above the squat tower of Lugwardine church and the more distant cathedral the Sugar Loaf and Skirrid and the dark ridge of the Black mountains merge into the background of Welsh hills.

At the field corner jink right and left and follow the hedge down, with a view over the village of Withington and its slender spire which catches the eye for miles around. Cross a stile, with the hedge now on the right, and walk down the small field to the road at Hynett Moor. Turn left for a few paces to a path on the right into the yard of Hynett Farm, where the dogs may be noisy. Do not be intimidated by the enclosed yard, but walk slightly left under the lean-to roof and go through a door.

Walk down the lawn and follow a hedge down to a gate and continue down a field to a footbridge close to where power lines converge with the stream. Cross the bridge, then railway tracks and another field to a hand gate, and follow a path along the edge of a garden to a road.

Turn right along the road for about 300 yards and near a red brick building cross to a foot path. Climb the slope of the field on a line to the right of a red brick house on the skyline and join a rough track.

Opposite the house turn right through a gap in the hedge and climb the field diagonally left converging with the hedge at the top and follow this to emerge onto another track. Cross this slightly left and walk down the field edge and at the bottom turn right into the adjoining field and descend steps into the village of Withington.

Walk along the village street for 200 yards to a bend and continue straight on, through a gate, on a track inclining away from the farm buildings at Stone House, to a road. Turn left and follow the road for almost a mile through a low lying area of Withington Marsh. *Withington - homestead among willows!*

Cross a stream and then the bed of the old Hereford and Gloucester canal, last encountered at Rudford. A little further, past the sandstone buildings of Lower House Farm turn right on a bridle-way passing Thing - hill Court.

Thing-hill Court and Thing-hill Grange are situated either side of Thing- hill a small round hill rising out of the surrounding lower fields. thing – Scandinavian council or public assembly?

Walk past farm buildings including two large broiler houses and turn left just before a final barn. After 100 yards the bridleway track turns and becomes a green lane for a short length and continues along the edge of three fields to Monkton Farm.

At the farm road the bridleway turns left while the Three Choirs Way continues straight across on a public footpath through the yard of the adjoining Old Monkton Farm. Past a barn and before the farm house turn right to a field gate and through this follow the field edge left to a stile in the corner.

Continue along the next field to a stile and footbridge where the public path forks right to Howberry Barn where another path crosses to a gate opposite the footbridge. As the field is usually grass there can be little objection to walking directly across it.

Through the gate follow the hedge to a further gate and the narrowing field rising to a stile in the highest corner from where a track leads through a gate to the road at Upper Castleton.

Turn left and walk around a sharp bend beneath large oak trees, and at the next bend join a footpath angling up the field to join a short length of green lane which emerges on to the village green at Ocle Pychard. *In old English, acleah – meaning a clearing in woodland. Recorded at Domesday as Acle. Roger Pichard, held the Manor in 1242, his name derives from pychard - old French for green woodpecker. The 13th Century church has a copper covered spire and three medieval bells, the earliest cast in Worcester in 1410.*

Edward Elgar

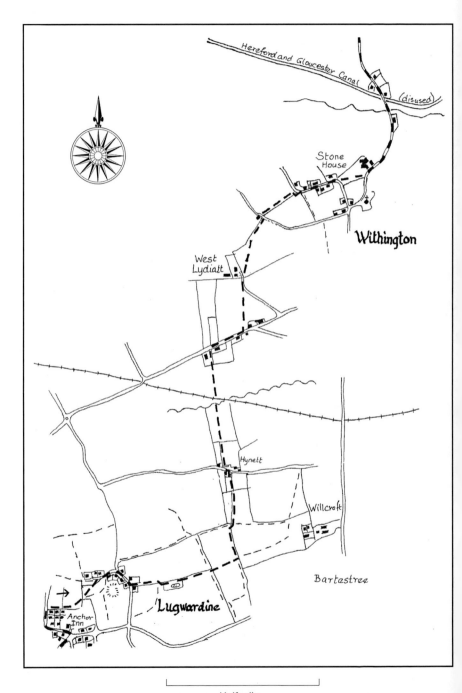

Half mile

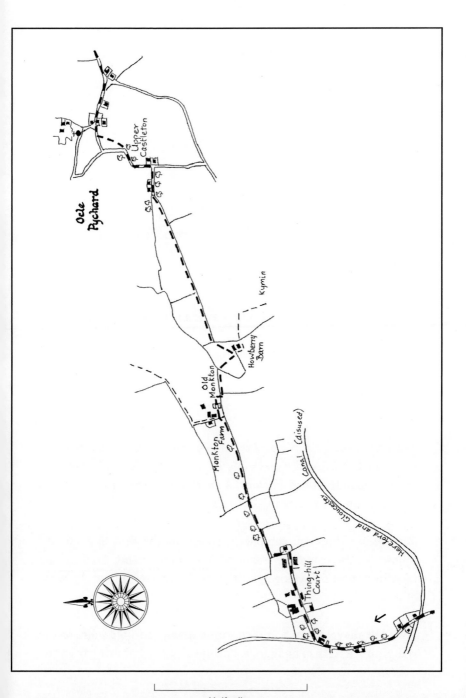

Ocle Pychard

Upper Castleton

Kymin

Howberry Barn

Old Monkton

Monkton Farm

Canal (disused)

Thing-hill Court

Hereford and Gloucester

Half mile

Much
Cowarne
Church

Ocle Pychard to Stanford Bishop

From the green turn right, passing a Victorian post box, and walk along the road for about three quarters of a mile, rising to give wide views of rural Herefordshire, to the Ledbury - Leominster road.

Turn right for 50 yards and cross to a bridleway along a track to Cowarne Court. As the track descends slightly the Malvern ridge shows above the trees in front. *A small circular building close to the woodland is a Norman dovecot.*

Just before the farm complex turn left at the first opportunity following the concrete road which bends right behind the buildings which have been built over the correct line of the right of way.

Fork left down a track and continue along the field edge to the remaining length of hedgerow. The path angles left away from the hedge towards the church tower and a stile in the next boundary - it may be more convenient to continue to the field corner.

Over the stile cross a low lying area to a footbridge and fork left up to a gate and walk beneath juniper and yew trees to the 14th century St Mary's church at Much Cowarne, - *old English - Cuaern, a cowhouse.*

Once the centre of a large and thriving community Cowarne was granted a Royal Charter in 1255 for a weekly market and annual fair. The church mound is said to have been a prehistoric fortification and later Norman hill fort.
The Three Choirs theme is maintained by the fact that Edward Elgar used to cycle the local lanes when visiting the church and friends at Cowarne Court. Shortly after visits here in 1901 he composed Pomp and Circumstance Number 1 and can we doubt that the countryside inspired England's unofficial anthem 'Land of Hope and Glory?

Leaving the church walk past the entrance gate to a kissing gate in the corner and turn right down a small field to exit through another gate and follow the church drive down to a road junction.

Continue straight on for about 400 yards to a gate on the left where a public footpath follows the line of the few remaining trees marking the old field boundary, after about 100 yards fork right following the tree line down to cross the River Lodon.

From the river walk straight across to a gateway and then follow the field edge to a stile and continue for about 100 yards before forking left over the slight rise to a gate. Farm buildings appear to have been built over the right of way at Hopes Rough Farm so cross the field well left of the farmhouse before forking right down to a gate onto the farm road.

Walk up to join a lane and follow it left around a sharp bend, past a footpath on the left, and continue up to a road. *There is a dearth of public paths in the vicinity where a route over Purley Hill directly in front would have been helpful. These quiet lanes must serve instead.*

Turn left along the road for 350 yards to a lane signposted to Stoke Lacy and follow it gently uphill and around several bends for another three quarters of a mile. Alongside the red bricked Hopton Villa turn right on a footpath climbing the slope past Hopton Court.

Through a gate the track levels and a panorama opens on the left extending to the shapely hills in the northwest including Croft Ambury, beyond Leominster.

Continue along the edge of two more fields before joining a short length of enclosed track. Past a house the track is private and the path continues through a gate and angles left up the field to re-join the track by a stile.

When the track shortly joins Stoke Lane follow this right for three quarters of a mile passing a footpath at Richley Farm but at Pembroke Lodge turn left through a gate and cross the field corner to a stile. Over this follow the hedge down, *with widening views over pastoral Herefordshire,* to a further stile and footbridge beneath large willow trees.

Through a gate in the next boundary hedge walk up a green lane to Munderfield Court with its surviving oast house. Then follow the surfaced farm track to the road at *Munderfield Row. - originally Mundell's Feld - a large cleared area of Forest.*

From the stile opposite, cross the field slightly left and walk down the hedge to a stile in a hollow. Climb the slope in the next field, again slightly left, to the ridge top and turn left on this broad viewpoint and walk down the ridge crossing several stiles to Upper Venn Farm. Walk to the right past a barn and join the farm track down to cross the River Frome, and then up to a road.

Turn left for 40 yards to a gate on the right where the path inclines away from the farm track following a shallow valley up to a stile in the hedge. Climb the slope slightly left up to a further stile and continue with the deep gully on the right to a gate into a small enclosure, sometimes muddy, and exit through a gate in the right hand corner.

Continue uphill past an electricity pole and bear left to a kissing gate and a route avoiding an enclosed farm yard. Follow the farm road past the farmhouse, The Hawkins, and through a gateway turn right down to a kissing gate and join the road at Stanford Bishop, *stoney ford - the Manor was held by the Bishop of Hereford.*

The church stands in isolation among a few trees on a slight rise just south of The Hawkins. It contains a medieval chair which has excited historians in the past, in the belief that it may have been used by St Augustin in 603 AD

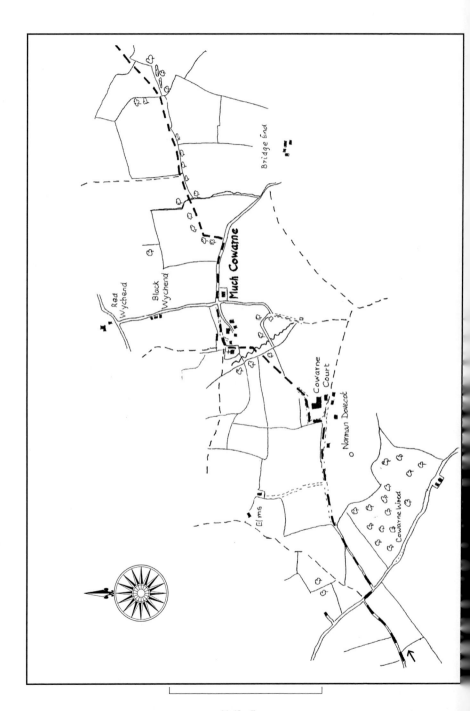

Half mile

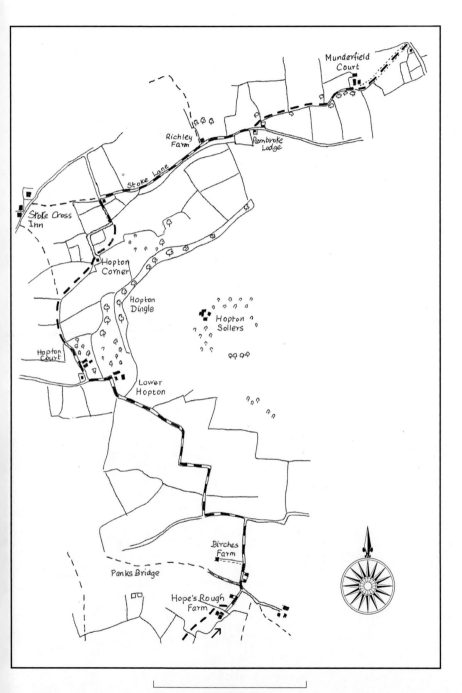

Munderfield
Court

Richley
Farm

Pembroke
Lodge

Stoke Lane

Stoke Cross
Inn

Hopton
Corner

Hopton
Dingle

Hopton
Sollers

Hopton
Court

Lower
Hopton

Birches
Farm

Panks Bridge

Hope's Rough
Farm

Half mile

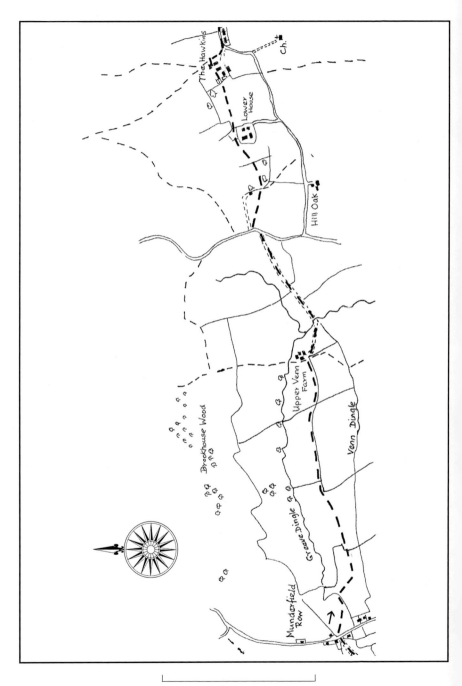

The Hawkins

Ch.

Lower House

Hill Oak

Brookhouse Wood

Upper Venn Farm

Venn Dingle

Greave Dingle

Munderfield Row

Half mile

Malvern Ridge

Stanford Bishop to Broad Green

Continue along the road for half a mile to the Bromyard- Malvern
road where the Herefordshire House Inn is 100 yards to the left.
Turn right, and after about 200 yards alongside a house, turn
left into a track which soon becomes a field edge path and, after
a short section, emerge at another road.

Turn left for about 200 yards to a track on the right alongside a
house and after 50 yards leave the track by a stile in the fence
and continue with the hedge on the left. After two further stiles
walk alongside a fence overlooking two small fishing lakes.

At the tail of the lakes ignore a stile in to woodland and turn left
across the dam and walk diagonally right up the next field to a
gate at the top corner. Through this follow the hedge down to a
plank bridge over a stream and a stile.

Follow the edge of the woodland for about a 100 yards and turn left on a cross path and continue up through the trees, crossing two more stiles, and entering Worcestershire.

Turn left along the field edge and around the corner follow the thick hedge, *the parish boundary between Linton and Suckley and the two counties.* After approximately 200 yards the path switches to the other side of the hedge and after crossing a track to Old Yearsett farm continues alongside a stream.

At the valley bottom cross the stream and from a gate walk uphill to Upper House. Follow a track to the left through a gate but just prior to a further gateway to a house, turn right over a stile. Walk up the hedge for 50 yards, with widening views over Herefordshire, and turn left over a further stile and walk up the field to a gate and continue up a grass slope to Knowl Farm. Cross the yard to a hand gate and emerge on to the road adjacent to the Cross Keys Inn.

From a stile opposite the pub angle left down the field to join a headland track alongside an orchard to a gate. Walk slightly right of a memorial oak down to a stile in the corner and over this follow the hedge for 50 yards to a further stile and then angle left down the next field to a road at Suckley Row.

The three counties were well known for their apples and the Worcester Pearmain, with its red streaked and juicy flesh, is archetypal.

Six thousand varieties once grew in Britain and are listed in the National Apple register and almost half are still available from the National Fruit Trials Centre at Brogdale in Kent, the world's most comprehensive apple collection.

The demise of apple varieties is blamed on the supermarkets who in turn blame customer demands for apples of uniform size, appearance and taste.

This led to the widespread loss of old orchards including cider and perry orchards which once enhanced many of the farms in the three counties.

There has recently been a resurgence of interest in growing traditional apples with grants available in some areas to encourage the planting of old varieties. 'Apple Fairs' are also increasingly popular autumn events, particularly in Herefordshire, so that in the future people may again be able to experience the range of flavours from the sharp and refreshing Beauty of Bath in August, to D'Arcy Spice which lived up to its name in spring.

Turn left down the road, crossing the bed of the disused railway, and turn right signposted Highfields. After about 100 yards turn left through a hand gate and cross a field to the remains of Old House Farm in woodland. Walk behind the ruin and descend steeply at first around a small coombe and then more gently through the wood. After a boggy area walk up to the edge of the wood and continue along the edge of the field to a road.

Cross to a gate alongside Coronation Cottage and follow the track to an old barn, turn right alongside a fence down to a stile, and continue down the field to the road. Cross over and descend, half left, to a stream and then climb the opposite side to the isolated church at Knightwick. Walk through the cemetery to a lane, turn left down to the road and cross to a footpath which contours to the right passing above a house to a gate. Cross a final field to reach the Worcester - Bromyard road at Knightwick.

Although this is not the most direct line for the Three Choirs Way between Hereford and Worcester, Knightwick is the most convenient crossing of the short but powerful river Teme. Rising in the Welsh hills the Teme flows past hop yards and orchards, farmsteads and hamlets and through the rich valley below the Abberley hills before rounding Ankerdine Hill towards the Severn.

Walk down the road 100 yards and cross the old road bridge over the Teme to the welcoming Talbot Inn. From the Inn walk up the hill signposted to Martley. The footway ends as the road steepens but around a bend turn off right onto a footpath climbing through woodland alongside a house. Follow the garden boundary turning left and climbing parallel with the road, at a path junction turn right more steeply uphill.

At the top of the steep section avoid a path cutting back left and continue alongside a palisade around a house, until reaching the ridge path and turn left. The path becomes a track and after about 300 yards, past a white gate at the wood edge, turn right close to a house. Access to the path is sometimes obscured by undergrowth but soon becomes a good track and lower, a pleasant hollow way.

Emerging from the woodland at a junction ignore a track forking right and continue down to a brick and clapboard barn and cross the stile alongside it. Descend steeply following a small valley curving right to a further stile and over this continue down a surfaced driveway. At the bottom keep left and turn left through a farm gate at Bannersbrook.

Cross the farmyard to a stile alongside a field gate and continue uphill at the edge of a wood. As the wood bends left continue directly uphill to a stile in the next hedge and from this angle left to a gate just left of a white cottage, and join Easinghope Lane.

This country differs from dry uplands, water hereabouts
is no white rarity. The muddy ditch
the Saxons named still moves beside the road
and milking-time soon churns the yard to sludge.

Men could build where they would; farms
five fields apart and cottages in threes up tracks
now detail slope and hollow, and lanes mizmaze
the countryside, hedges a screen for lover and for fox.

Thorn, hazel, briar make them alike, easy
to lose one's way, different in small things only -
empty beehives in a gangling orchard, a church
with no apparent parish, shock-yewed and lonely.

Sometimes these lanes go by, irrelevant as thoughts,
for miles with only magpies, padlocked gate, and crop,
a philosophic pattern to the man born locally,
to others only metaphors without a map.

Molly Holden

Turn right down the lane to a junction and converted oast-houses, at Doddenham. Follow the wall left for a few yards to a footpath on the right and over an awkward stile, walk down alongside a fence before turning left following the valley.

Through a gateway continue following the valley up to the field boundary of old willow trees and continue alongside it to a gate and cross the next field, passing under power lines, to a lane.

Turn right and after 50 yards join a track on the left which roughly parallels the power lines. Where the track eventually bends right continue across the open field following the power lines to the corner of a wood and continue along the wood edge for about 100 yards. As both the wood and power lines bend away left continue straight down the sloping field to a footbridge hidden under the trees.

In the next field, incline right and follow the hedge line over stiles in to Broad Green.

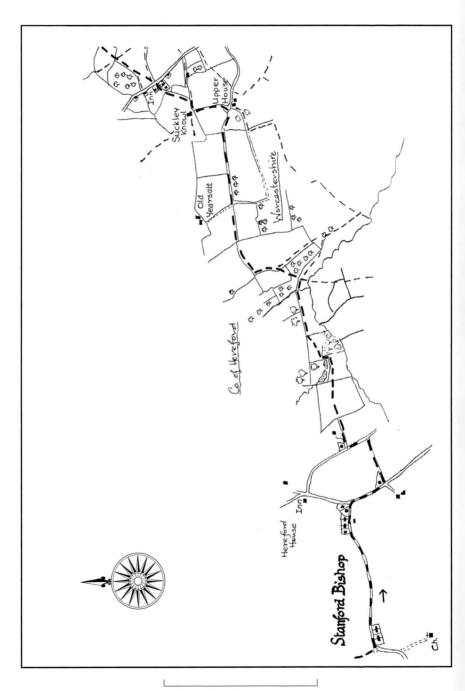

Half mile

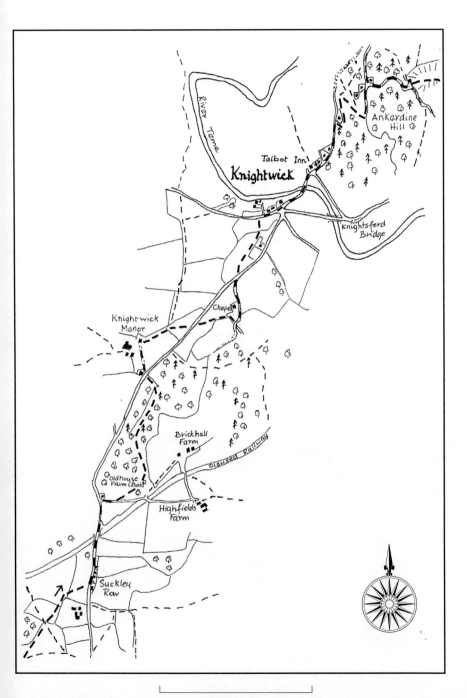

Half mile

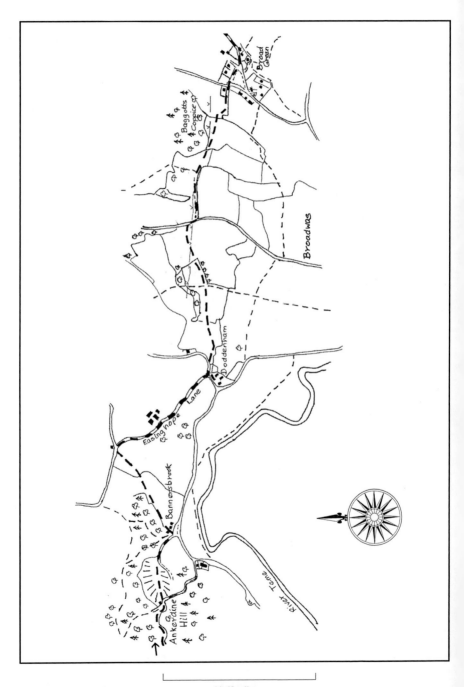

Half mile

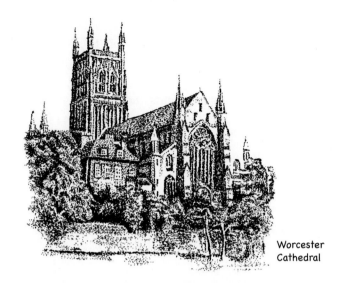

Worcester
Cathedral

Broad Green to Stanbrook

Cross a road to a track along the side of the village green and past a farm entrance turn left on a narrow lane which soon becomes a rough track. After a 150 yards, just before gates, turn right over a stile and follow the headland towards woodland.

At the field corner, turn right for 50 yards and then left to a pedestrian gate, sometimes hidden in undergrowth. Through this emerge into an open field and follow the wood edge to the left through three fields. After the third stile turn right passing the remains of Blackfield Cottage and a pond on the left and at the field corner turn left to a further stile. Over this follow the field edge to further stiles either side of a thick hedge and cross the next field parallel with the hedge to the right.

Cross a narrow footbridge and a stile and then a line of oak trees marking an old field boundary to a gate in the corner alongside a small enclosure. Through the gate follow the field edge to a stile and cross the next small field to a footbridge and hand gate. Again follow the hedge on the left to the field corner and go through the left of two gates, then turn right over a stile and footbridge.

Walk along the edge of two fields and from the second gate angle left up the field in line with the nearest houses to a gate on to the road at Upper Broadheath. Turn right and after a cross-road continue for about 400 yards to the Plough Inn and adjacent Elgar Centre - a path along the edge of the common is preferable to using the road.

A few yards past the pub the Three Choirs main route follows a bridleway left alongside the garden of Elgar's birthplace.

Elgar was born at The Firs, Upper Broadheath, now a museum housing a collection of priceless manuscripts, including many of his original scores. The cottage has a very welcoming aura and Elgar often alluded to this and his awareness that 'music is in the air around you'.

This alternative route avoiding the city and is same distance

Continue along the road for about fifty yards to a footpath on the right and follow the thick hedge and stream, an ancient parish boundary, down through several fields to the A44 road.

Turn left and cross to Otherton Lane and follow it for half a mile. At sharp bend continue on a footpath down the steep slope and from a stile at the bottom cross the next two fields diagonally to the road at Bransford Bridge over the river Teme.

Cross the bridge and the road to a lane alongside the Fox Inn and follow it for over half a mile and at a sharp right bend join a footpath on the left adjacent to the entrance to Bransford Court.

The path allows a fine view of the Court and landscaped lake and joins a farm track which converges with the Teme again turns right. After a 100 yards go left through a gate and walk alongside the river until it ends left, then continue alongside a patchy hedgerow for about 60 yards to a hunt gate.

This leads to open access land and some walkers tend to follow the river bank but the more direct route is across the water meadows of a single tree towards the tall chimney at Powick and a footbridge in the next hedge boundary.

Cross the next field to a stile about 60 yards from a white house visible among the trees on the right. From the stile turn half right to a gate and stile at the edge of the woodland. Climb the steep slope and follow the path left along the scarp *with views to the cathedral and Glover's Needle seen over the trees to the left.*

At Powick use a pedestrian crossing slightly left to cross a busy road to an unsigned track which climbs and passes houses to become a narrow path leading to a kissing gate into the churchyard. Pass the church tower (to visit the village pub turn right through the lychgate) and follow the boundary fence on the right between yew trees and laurel bushes to a kissing gate.

Cross a narrow field to a gate and follow the hedge beyond rising slightly above the surrounding fields before dropping down to a cross path at a hedge and stream. Turn left passing under power lines to a gate and continue curving right to a footbridge to join the main route of the Three Choirs Way coming from Worcester.

With the main route follow the track for about half a mile to Oldbury Farm and after two bridlegates continue directly towards the cathedral tower.

The bulk of Bredon Hill also looms and beyond is the high blue edge of Cotswold. To the right, the Malvern ridge extends southwards.

The bridleway soon becomes a surfaced lane and at a sharp bend joins Oldbury Road which is followed for about a mile and a half to the banks of the Severn. Any tedium of walking though the suburb might be relieved at the Copper Top Inn. Otherwise continue and after crossing Henwyck Road descend Holywell Hill to reach the west bank of the river. Turn right for 200 yards to the Sabrina footbridge and cross the river.

Turn right on the riverside path, part of the Severn Way long distance path, and from the end of Worcester Bridge continue pleasantly along the riverside walk passing the Glovers's Needle. *This slender spire of St Andrew's, rising to 245 feet, commemorates the Worcester glove trade, which up to 1800 gave employment to 8000 people in the city and surrounding countryside.*

After 300 yards the medieval Portway leads up to the Cathedral, and the city centre. *Note the floodwater levels on the embankment which show why the Three Choirs Way may not be accessible at all times of the year!*

Completed in 1998, the Severn Way runs for 220 miles, along or near the river, from the source on Plynlimon to the sea. A mountain torrent in parts of Powys the river meanders through Shropshire and Worcestershire past historic scenes and ancient communities. The river changes from tree bordered tranquillity at Tewkesbury, to a mile wide tidal estuary at Sheperdine before joining the Bristol Channel.

The Severn is Britains longest river. Rising in the mountains of mid Wales, close to the source of the Wye, the two rivers enclose a tract of countryside as attractive as any in the country, aptly described as 'blessed is the eye between Severn and Wye'.

A crucial trade route for centuries, by the 1600s the Severn was the second busiest river in Europe, after the Meuse. In 1701 there was a regular water taxi between Shrewsbury and Gloucester, and , by the middle of the 18th Century, 100,000 tons of coal was shipped down the river from Coalport annually. Severn Trows of up to 80 tons laden, plied both up and downstream to adjacent Midland towns, the Bristol Channel ports, and beyond.

The city arose around a major ford when the Severn was still tidal up to this point. The strong Saxon influence - the west Saxons here were prominent in the defeat of the Danes- led to the Shire system developing in England. In the Fifth Century Worcester was the fifth city in the land.

After the Norman Conquest Worcester was the only diocese to retain a Saxon Bishop, Wulfstan.

King John visited Worcester in 1206 claiming it to be his favourite city and in his will requested burial there. He is said to have been influenced by a prophesy, attributed to Merlin, that he would eventually rest among Saints. Subsequently, his tomb between that of St Oswald and St Wulfstan led to Worcester becoming a centre of pilgrimage, with resulting wealth, a century before Gloucester found similar fame and fortune.

The Civil War began and ended at Worcester. In 1642 royalists were recruiting in the area, generally loyal to the king, when a skirmish at Powick Bridge resulted in the Parliamentary force being routed by royal cavalry under Prince Rupert.

Throughout the fluctuating fortunes of the war Worcester

remained under a royal garrison until 1651 when the last engagement of the conflict also took place at Powick where Cromwell's forces utilised a pontoon bridge to breach the city's defences. Final retribution, Cromwell's 'Crowning Mercy', resulted in the destruction of the massive, 50' high, city walls.

John Wesley looked with affection on "our lovely and loving people of Worcester, plain, old genuine Methodists"!

William Cobbett, reporting the state of agricultural England in 1826, found it "one of the cleanest, neatest and handsomest towns I ever saw, indeed I do not recollect to have seen any one equal....the town is precisely in character with the beautiful and rich country in which it lies".
Elgar lived with his parents in Worcester from 1859 to 1879, where his fathers music shop was at 10 High Street. After the death of his wife Elgar returned to live in Kempsey near Worcester from 1929 until his death in 1934.

Continue, southwards, on the Severn Way for over two miles, passing the entrance to the Birmingham canal at Diglis Basin and then Diglis lock to the Severn. After a length of rural riverside a side stream blocks the way necessitating a short diversion inland to a footbridge and return to the river bank to continue southwards.

Shortly after passing the confluence with the River Teme on the opposite bank, walk past a chalet holiday park with Carrington Road Bridge looming in front. Just before reaching the bridge leave the river on a public foot path which passes in front of the Site office and ascends the slope behind to emerge alongside the Ketch Inn (now a Toby Carvery).

Turn right on the cycle/walk way to the bridge and continue as it crosses high above the river with wide views to the Teme and the site of the civil war Battle of Worcester of 1651.

There was Welsh in the English water
That flowed from distant mountains
Where high on Plynlimon springs the Hafren.
There hawk, the buzzard and the merlin,
Westward hovers Cader Idris
And the silver Dovey.
The rushing stream passes
Through peat and pool,
Waterfall and cascade,
Spouts to Llyn Crochan,
Then sliding to Blaen Hafren
Becomes the Severn.
. . . To enter gorge and wood
To wind by castle, hill, and valley,
Meander through remote pastures
Then race through towns and under bridges
To Bewdley, Stourport, Worcester, . . .
Past Callow End, past Kempsey church
That looks from its hill across the Ham
Over shoals and willows to the Old Hills
And the blue line of the Malverns.
Downstream lie Severn Stoke and Pixham Ferry,
Its rusted chains now vanished,
No longer used to haul across the hunt.
Farther down lie Upton,
Ripple with its misericords . . .
Then Tewkesbury, Gloucester,
The estuary and the Bristol Channel. . .

Robin Ivy

In about three hundred yards turn right on to a track descending back towards the river. Turn right at the bottom and pass under the bridge to a gate into the riverside fields. Through the gate angle left passing close to large oak trees to a further gate at the far side of the field.

Although this is access land where the public are entitled to walk, there is no obligation for the highway authority to erect signs or provide means of access. In climbing over gates and fences there is an onus on walkers to ensure that no damage is caused.

An alternative to using this route is to continue along the river bank for about 600 yards and after crossing a stile in a small copse, turn right over a further stile on a footpath leading to the same point.

In the next field the path gradually converges with a stream on the left and after another gate continue until the stream and power lines converge and turn left over a stile and a footbridge into an enclosed track. The alternative route from Broadheath joins from the right

Near a house the right of way has been diverted over a footbridge and continues inside the field to a stile.

In the next field pass the heavily noduled trunk of an oak and from the next hedge angle right across the field close to another large oak to a stile onto a road.

Cross the road with care as foliage may obscure you from approaching drivers and enter an enclosed path through a metal kissing gate.

Stanbrook Abbey, on the other side of the hedge, was occupied until recently by a community of Benedictine nuns and was the home of the oldest private printing press in England. The Abbey Press was established in 1876 and the only private press from the nineteenth century still working in the twenty first.

* * *

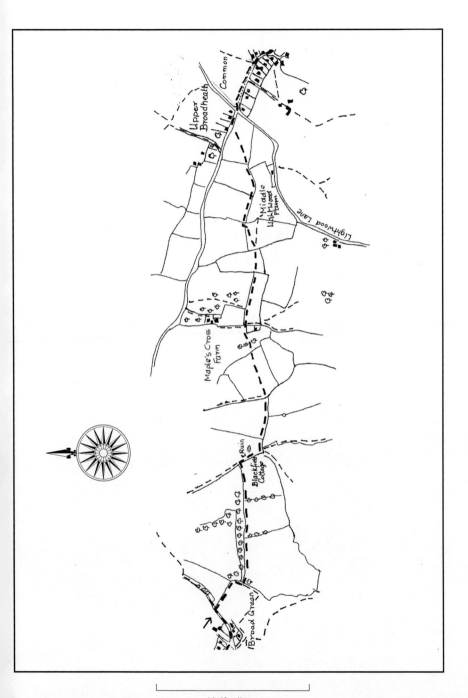

Common

Upper
Broadheath

Middle
Lightwood
Farm

Lightwood Lane

Maple's Cross
Farm

Ruin

Blackfield
Cottage

Broad Green

Half mile

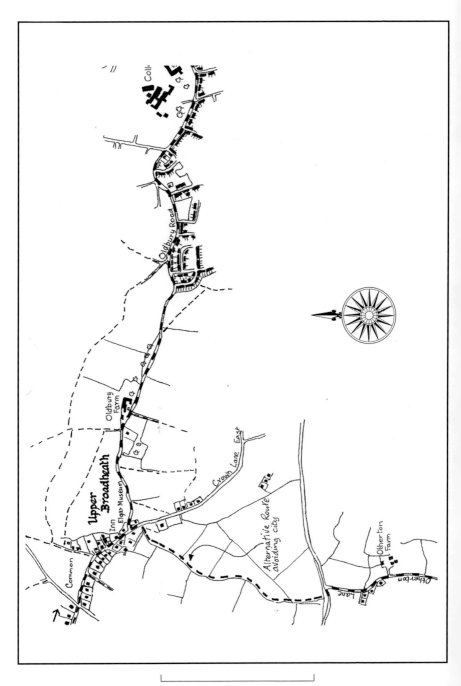

Half mile

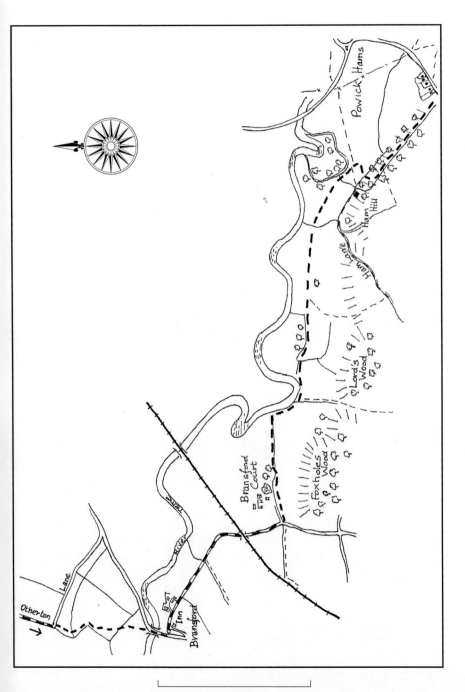

Half mile

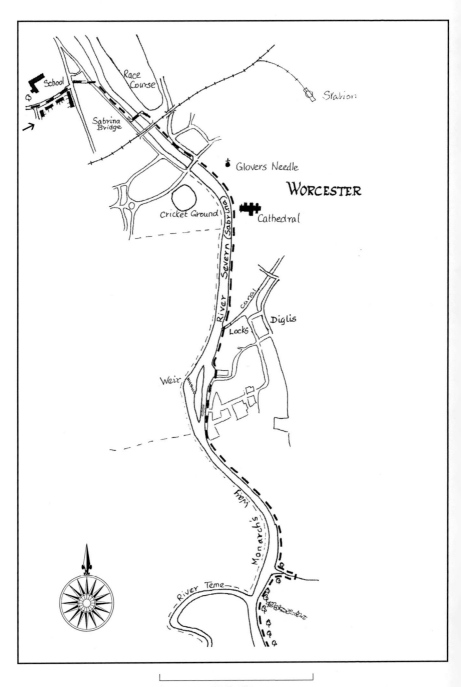

Half mile

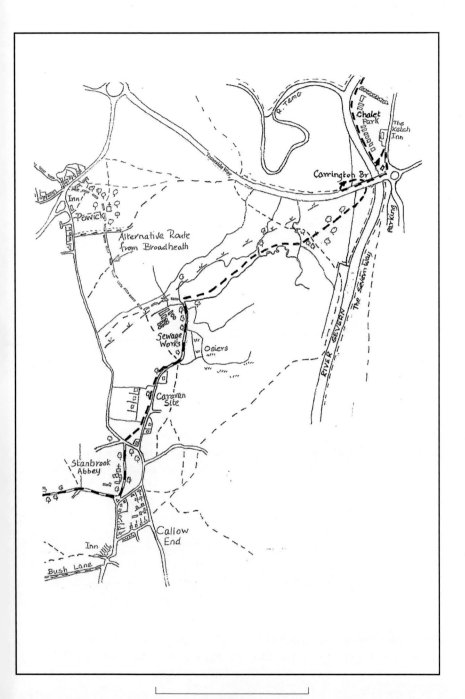

Half mile

Worcester Beacon

Stanbrook Abbey to British Camp

Emerge from the path close to the village of Callow End, and the
Bluebell Inn is a short distance further along the main road.

*Calwa – a bare hillside – refers to the Old Hills which are still
largely bare of trees. The village was a centre of hop growing up
to the 1950s when itinerant pickers descended on the village
in considerable numbers.*

> The barley grows with modest head,
> The hop is all ambition,
> But when in barrels they are wed
> The mixture is perfection.
> Hail to thee, Worcestershire!
>
> *George Griffith*

Turn right along a lane between a hedge and high brick wall for
about 300 yards. As the lane curves left continue over a stile in

to a green track which climbs to join a hard track near stables. Continue straight to the ridge top and a view back to Powick Church.

The path diverts past a house down to a stile and choice of paths. Follow the hedge to the left down through two paddocks to a stile in to access land and take any route to the summit of the Old Hills and a splendid panorama – *north to the Cathedral and Glovers Needle, and further east the Severn Vale. In the west the Suckley Hills are overshadowed by North Hill at the end of the Malvern ridge.*

From the concrete Trig. Pillar, conversely just below the highest point, walk down a broad path to the remains of a boundary fence. The path continues as a bridleway but at the edge of the trees leave the track and fork left on a footpath crossing the field towards woodland.

Follow a path through the wood to an exit stile and turn right through a gate and then immediately left along the field edge to a stream, the Madresfield Brook and through a gate follow the wooded bank of the stream to the right for about a mile.

Approaching parkland around Madresfield Court angle away from the stream to a gate and join a surfaced lane. Walk beneath a variety of mature trees and exit past the Lodge, with its particularly splendid chimney, to a road. *Madresfield Court mentioned in a charter of Henry I has been occupied by descendants of the same family since 1160.*

Turn left, and after 50 yards cross the road to a path through a gate. Cross the short field close to a childrens play area and from a kissing gate follow a track alongside the hedge down to a gate and stile.

Continue alongside the hedge to a kissing gate into woodland and follow the wood edge to a road. Cross to a path up the middle of a field and after several fences and a roadside copse reach a road bypassing Malvern Link.

Over the road the path continues alongside industrial warehouse units, crossing a service road, until confronted by an electricity sub-station. Follow a path left and then right over a concrete slab footbridge to reach the front of the sub-station.

Turn left and walk up the access road, keep left at a junction, and continue past a sports field to a T junction.

Cross over, slightly right, to an enclosed path between hedges. When the path ends cross the road on to Malvern Link common *where an encircled hawthorn tree offers an excuse for a brief pause*. Walk uphill inclining left though trees and shrubbery to an underpass in the embankment of the Hereford to Worcester railway line. Cross a narrow road and continue up the steepening Common, still inclining left, to the Nags Head Inn and then continue up the narrow Bank Street alongside the pub.

Emerge onto North Malvern Road under the steep slopes of North Hill and cross to the opposite pavement and follow it left for about 300 yards where a public footpath commences inside a private looking drive. The path lacks a signpost and might easily be missed. House numbers 59,61,63 at the entrance and Oriel House with ornate pinnacles on the opposite side of the road are landmarks. Inside the driveway cross to steep stone steps signposted to North Hill.

> *It is difficult to describe or recommend any particular route along the switchback of the Malvern Hills in detail. The open grassy contours have many paths and tracks at different levels which allow routes to be chosen at will.*

From North Hill the ridge drops then climbs to a Topograph on the summit of Worcester Beacon from which it is two miles to the Wyche Cutting, a narrow pass through the hills and route of an ancient Salt Way from Droitwich and a further three miles to British Camp an extensive hill fort on Hereford Beacon the second highest point on the ridge.

Urban Malvern clusters at different levels along the eastern flank of the hills, spreading south from North Malvern through Malvern Link to the centre of Great Malvern set below North Hill.

Slightly detached, and almost half way down the length of the ridge, is Malvern Wells, where Holy Well derived its name from the miraculous cures attributed to bathing in the water and Eye Well is recorded in 1622 being a cure for sore eyes.

Malvern water has been famous for centuries. Whilst springs all over Europe are well known for their mineral content Malvern water is reputed because of its purity.

The small cottage at St Ann's Well, built in 1815, is a memorial to the original 'village spa' which existed before the water cures achieved national acclaim and the wealthy influx brought the large houses, hotels and the Promenade Gardens. In 1781 the water sold in London at one shilling a bottle and is still marketed commercially from St Johns Well.

After his marriage in 1889, Edward Elgar and his wife lived in the London area for two, fairly unproductive years. In 1891 they returned to live in Great Malvern, firstly in Alexandra Road and then in Wells Road, where Elgar's study overlooked the wide panorama of the Severn Vale.

The hills, over which Elgar regularly wandered, were a constant source of inspiration to him and he completed the 'Enigma Variations', 'The Dream of Gerontius', and the 'Pomp and Circumstance Marches' during this period.

The Malvern Hills, consisting of complex and exceptionally hard rocks which has resisted natural erosion for at least 650 million years, run north - south for over 10 miles rising to a height of 1394 feet at Worcester Beacon. Much of the ridge is dry grassland with patches of bilberry and heather and is designated an Area of Outstanding Natural Beauty.

The hills are protected by law incorporating a Board of Conservators who manage and maintain the environment of the hills and surrounding commons, a major function being the preservation of public accessibility. Fewer sheep now graze the hills than previously, allowing woodland and scrub to extend, while regular, managed, burning brings fresh growth with a legacy of native wildflowers, including bluebells and foxgloves. Lower slopes are clad in low scrub, blackberry, bracken, broom and gorse with areas of woodland consisting of silver birch, mountain ash, hawthorn, sycamore and, lower still, oak.

The entire area, including the adjoining commons, is open to the public and criss crossed by a network of paths and tracks estimated at more than 100 miles in extent. Through walkers, and first time visitors, may wish to walk the backbone of the ridge. Others will prefer lower levels, walking through primrose and bluebells in spring and tree shade in summer, or taking the waters at St Anne's Well.

....."twelve fair counties saw the glare from Malverns lonely peak", according to Macaulay in his poem on the Spanish Armada. Others claim as many as fifteen. However many the panorama is magnificent and on a clear day extends beyond the three counties.

Eastward across the Severn vale is the blue Cotswold horizon, southward the lower Severn and Bristol Channel show clearly. In the west the undulating and well wooded hills of Herefordshire continue to the mountains of Brecon and Radnor.

The Shire Ditch is a prominent feature of the ridge top. In 1290 Gilbert de Clare, Earl of Gloucester constructed this boundary between his land and that of the Bishop of Hereford. Craftily, it was said, so that deer could jump easily from west to east but with considerably more difficulty the opposite way!

The ridge narrows to the pass at British Camp where Little Malvern and the remains of the Benedictine Priory can be glimpsed below.

William Langland was born at Ledbury and educated at Little Malvern Priory where he may have written part of his famous allegorical poem "The vision of Piers Plowman". From the Norman Conquest the Saxon tongue was declining and soon, with much of France owing allegiance to England, French nobility and their entourage were commonplace at the English Court. After 250 years the two languages were beginning to coalesce. Langland's literature was part of an important revival of the native tongue, and his idiomatic use of English was the base for the language of Shakespeare.

* * *

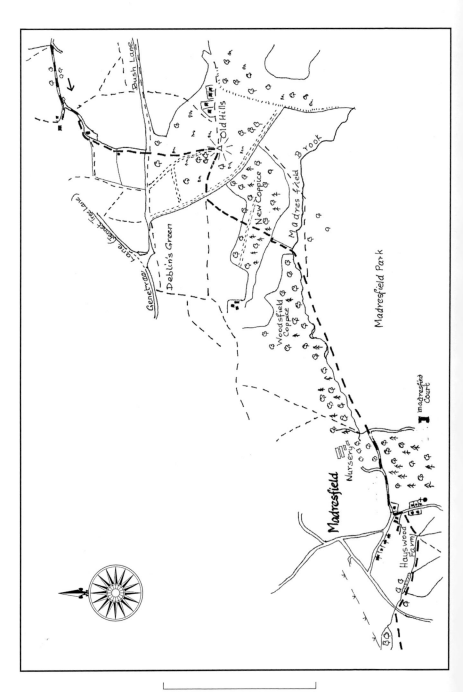

Half mile

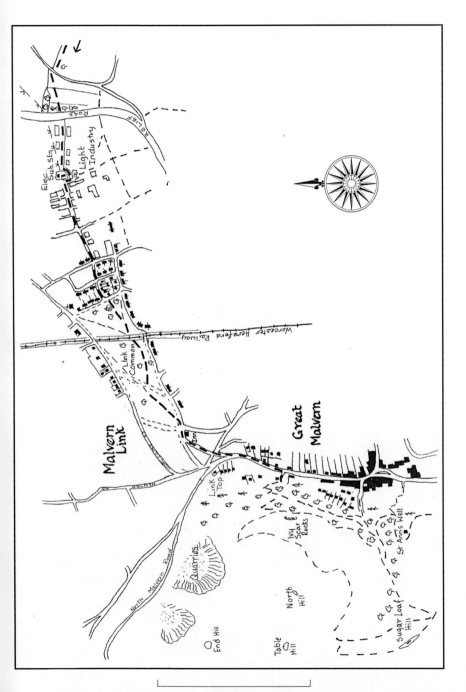

Half mile

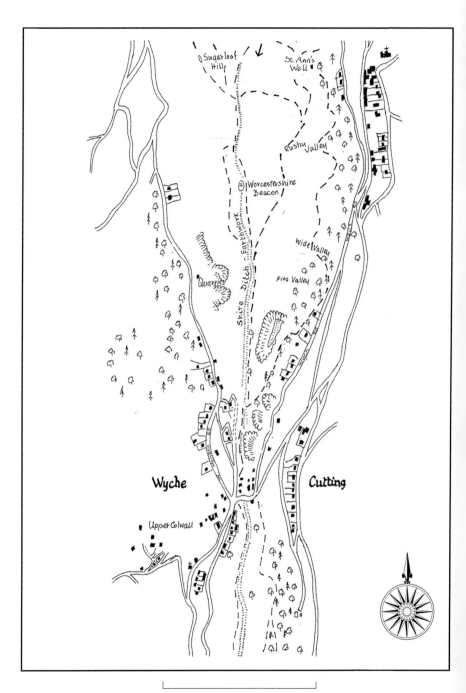

Sugarloaf Hill

St Ann's Well

Rushy Valley

Worcestershire Beacon

Shire Ditch Earthwork

Wide Valley

Fits Valley

Quarries

Wyche

Cutting

Upper Colwall

Half mile

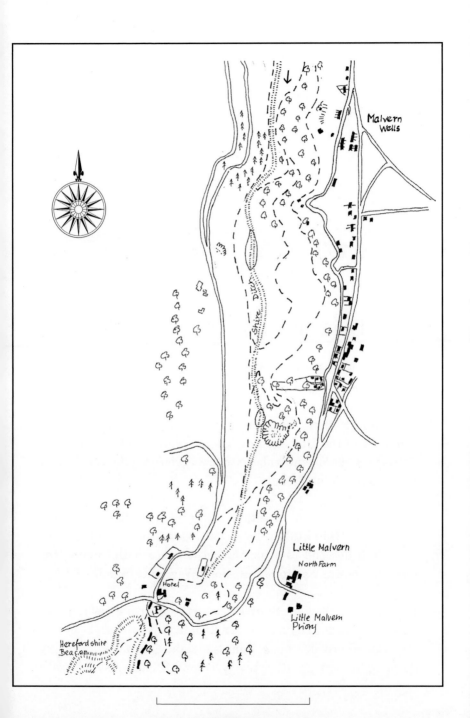

Half mile

Distant Cotswold scarp

British Camp to Staunton

From the British Camp Hotel cross the road and bear right in
the car park to a gate and path to Herefordshire Beacon. In a few
yards the path forks and some walkers of the Three Choirs Way
will choose to climb the steep path to the right to the impressive
ramparts of the Iron age fort. The more direct route continues
contouring more gently above the reservoir to gain the ridge at
Broad Down in half a mile.

From a signpost cairn either continue with the ridge over
Hangman's Hill or take a lower path along the edge of the tree
line. Both descend to a narrow col where a path, linking the
Gloucestershire Way to Three Choirs Way, joins from the left.

From the col follow the Shire Ditch up the steep narrow ridge for
about 100 yards and just before a final high point with brambles
and blackthorn intruding from the right, join a path angling
down right through attractive woodland. If you miss this path

continue with the ridge and turn down the slope at the next opportunity.

The path joins a track which descends through Gullet Wood. *An anomaly perhaps, is that the track although immediately adjacent to the Malvern Hills AONB, is used as a test track for off road vehicles which results in the track being deeply rutted and very muddy at times.*

After a gate and cattle grid walkers can make use of a path in the wood alongside the track to avoid the worst of any mud. From the next path junction the prominent Obelisk overlooking Eastnor Castle and its parkland can be visited, otherwise continue up the flank of Midsummer Hill followed by a gradual descent to Hollybush on the Tewkesbury - Ledbury road.

Turn left over the crest and descend for about 200 yards to a track on the right just before a telephone kiosk. The track climbs bending left and right around a low shoulder where a steep path up the ridge allows a traverse of both Ragged Stone and Chase End Hills if desired.

Otherwise continue on the track which levels out through deciduous woodland but after about 350 yards leave this pleasant way and turn left down to an obvious gate.

Walk down the open field, angling right about 45 degrees to a track and through a gate continue through thick woodland and soon crossing a bridge over the narrow road leading to Whiteleaved Oak.

Continue for half a mile to a point where the track curves left then right and a cross track descends from the right. Follow this track left down through a field gate and continue, close to a large oak tree, down the field edge with wide views to Bredon Hill and other Cotswold outliers.

At the road, Chase End Street, turn right passing a turning to Camer's Green and at a bend turn left on a footpath alongside the thatched Hawthorn Cottage. Follow the hedge down the field and as it bends right pass through a wide gap to the left of a small pond and with the hedge now on the right, continue to a footbridge. *The pond is one of thirty or more in the close vicinity and indicates why this particular field is often very wet.* From the footbridge walk up the field angling slightly right towards a line of four oak trees where a slightly raised track leads to a gate onto a road.

Established by William the Conqueror in 1083, as Royal Hunting Forest, Malvern Chase extended as heath and woodland from the banks of the Severn.

Turn right for about 200 yards to a footpath through a gate on the left and follow the hedge to a stile. Walk down the next field edge past a barn to a further stile and cross the field to a gate, right of a house, onto Cook's Lane. Follow the lane left for half a mile to a junction and turn right for another half mile, passing under the M50, and alongside the Wyndbrook to a T junction at Pendock.

Turn left towards the village, which has a shop and Post Office, but in 50 yards turn right through a field gate. Walk up the centre of the field to a second gate and from this angle left to a footbridge in the hedge to the left and continue up the next field alongside the hedge and turn right at the top.

The wide view from this slight vantage point includes a glimpse of May Hill summit over the trees in front, and Gadsbury Bank off to the left, its ancient fortifications shrouded by the tree cover. Over your shoulder the Malvern ridge stretches northward.

Follow the field edge to a stile and continue with the hedge on the right to a road at Dobshill. Turn right past the farm buildings to a stile on the left and walk around the buildings, and under a horse chestnut tree, to a gate with a gap alongside. Now follow a splendid ridge path for three quarters of a mile.

Trees obscure the view westwards but to the east Gadsbury Bank and the cone shape of Berth Hill stand out in the vale with the spire of Eldersfield Church between them.

Reaching a hunt gate turn left and follow the boundary hedge down and go through the right hand of two gates. Turn right following the hedge *with an imposing Gothic pile, which was once Staunton vicarage, on the other side.*

Cross a lane and continue rising towards Staunton Coppice to a gate onto a farm track. Follow it left but after 100 yards turn right through a gate and walk up the field parallel to a woodland on the right to a further gate under an oak tree. Continue alongside the hedge but at the end of the woodland and before the next cross hedge turn right over a stile.

On the other side of the hedge turn left along the edge of a garden to a junction with a stoned track and turn right. Where the track turns left continue along an enclosed grassy path passing a bungalow and outbuildings and sometimes tethered goats.

Cross a stile part of the local Whitmore Way, and turn left on a cross bridleway. Through a hunt gate walk along an enclosed length of track to Moat Lane and follow it right to the Gloucester to Ledbury road at Staunton.

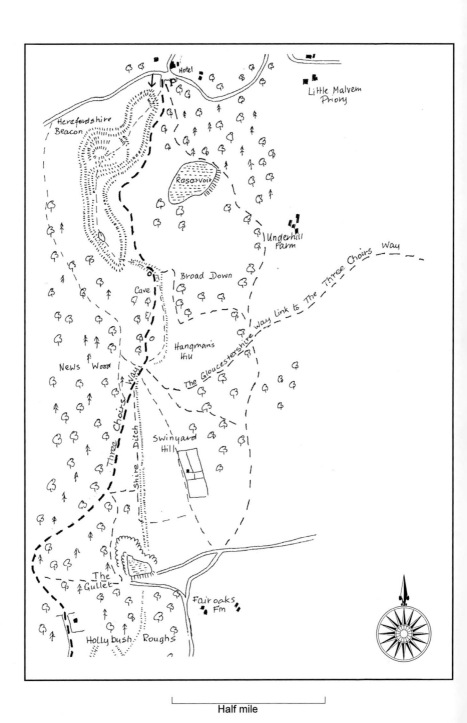

Hotel

Little Malvern
Priory

Herefordshire
Beacon

Reservoir

Underhill
Farm

Broad Down

Cave

The Gloucestershire Way link to The Three Choirs Way

Hangman's
Hill

News Wood

Three Choirs Way

Shire Ditch

Swinyard
Hill

The
Gullet

Fairoaks
Fm

Hollybush Roughs

Half mile

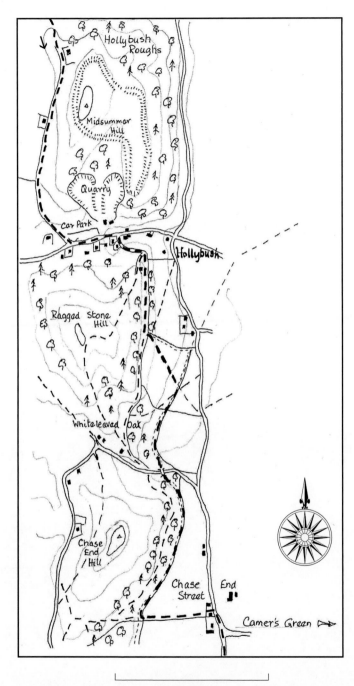

Half mile

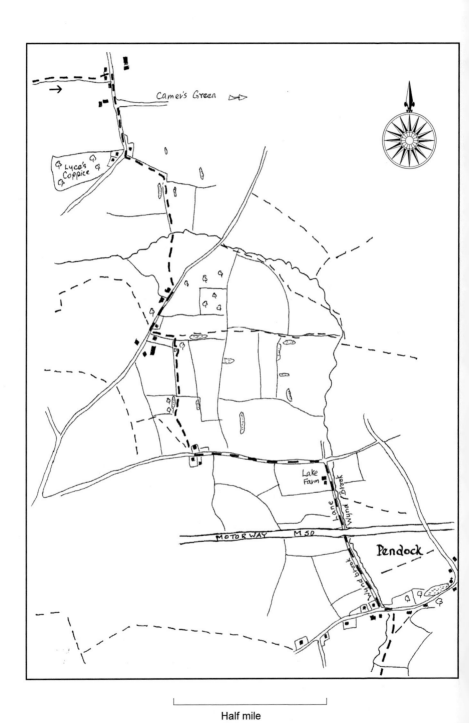

Camer's Green

Lyce's Coppice

Lake Farm

Lane

Wynd Brook

MOTORWAY   M 50

Pendock

Wynd Brook

Half mile

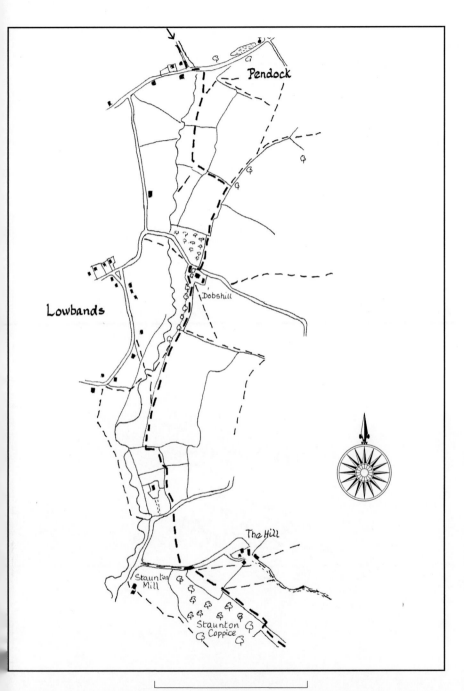

Pendock

Lowbands

Dobshill

The Hill

Staunton
Mill

Staunton
Coppice

Half mile

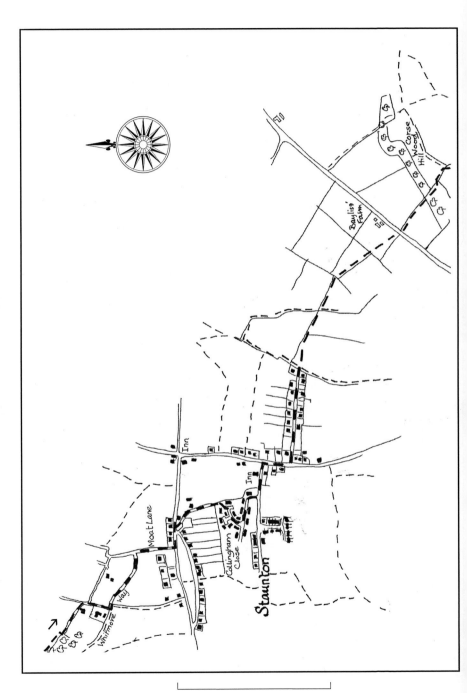

Half mile

Gloucester
Cathedral

Staunton to Gloucester Cathedral

Turn left along the road for 100 yards and cross to a footbridge where an enclosed path is followed around the edge of paddocks to Collingham Close. Turn left at the next two road junctions and shortly pass the Prince of Wales Inn.

The Chartist movement campaigned for electoral reform including enfranchisement for women long before such radical ideas became acceptable. One enthusiast, Feargus O'Connor, planned to encourage downtrodden industrial workers back to the land and purchased farms at Lowbands and Staunton which were divided into 2,3 and 4 acre plots. Each was provided with a four roomed bungalow of identical design and the project included a pub, The Prince of Wales, an enlarged design of the bungalows, and a village school at Lowbands. Unfortunately few members were able to sustain themselves from their plots or to pay their first annual rents. The project collapsed with Feargus O'Connor bankrupted but the buildings survive and many are now listed buildings.

At the T junction turn right and after 150 yards left in to School Crescent - *consisting of Chartist bungalows set in their unusually large plots.* At the road end climb a stile and walk across the field converging with the hedge on the left in about 100 yards.

Pass through a gap in the next hedge near a large oak tree and continue, still with the hedge on the left, over a foot bridge and along the next field to a stile alongside a gate.
Follow the hedge on the right to a stile and in the next field bear right to a footbridge in the corner on to the road between Gloucester and Upton on Severn.

Cross to a gate opposite and walk up the field to a stile and continue steeply up alongside Corse Wood. At the top go through a gate on the left, again with a stile alongside, and turn right following the hedge downhill for about 200 yards to a stile. Over this continue down, now with the hedge to the left, to a gate onto a lane.

Turn right, and after about 50 yards, left on a footpath down the driveway at Ivy Cottage. As the drive bends left to the cottage, walk straight on, past a garage and between vegetable plots to a stile. Bear left to a further stile, over this continue with the hedge to the left. After 150 yards or so fork left through a gate near an electricity pole. *Barrow Hill imitates May Hill in profile and further off Sandhurst Hill on the Severn stands out against the blue line of the Cotswolds.*

Follow the line of the electricity poles down to a stile alongside Lime Kiln Farm on to a lane. Turn right for about 40 yards to a bridleway on the left and cross the field to a gate where the bridleway forks left, but continue on a footpath down a good track with the hedge to the left. At the bottom of this field stay on the track bending left through a coppice of poplar trees and past the remains of Foscombe Farm. *Foscombe House, a Gothic extravaganza built by Thomas Fulljames in 1840, can be glimpsed on Foscombe Hill up to the right.*

The track passes through a gap in a cross hedge but in 100 yards, at a path junction, turn left over the stream, and then immediately right following it. Cross a stile and walk along the field where the abundant ash and willow trees obscure surrounding views other than Sandhurst Hill in front over the trees.

Pass a field gate on the right and after another 150 yards, just prior to power lines, turn right through a farm gate and over a culvert. Walk up the field, moving away from the hedge slightly, to a stile in to a coppice and follow either of two public ways which cross the playing field either in front or behind the white painted pavilion.

Past the pavilion turn right along an enclosed path between houses to a road and turn left to a T junction in the centre of Ashleworth.

While there are many rights of way in the vicinity of the village few lead satisfactorily towards Gloucester. Two routes are suitable for the Three Choirs Way, but in the event of winter flooding neither will be passable on foot and it would be necessary to stay on the road from Ashleworth along the ridge to Maisemore.

Alternative Route following the bank of the Severn
From the T junction, cross to a track to the right of the Post Office and follow it for a few yards and then cross a stile on the right. Walk diagonally down the field, passing left of a row of specimen field trees, Field Maple, Black

---

Poplar, Copper Beech Common Lime and Hornbeam, and through a gap at the corner. Continue on the same line in the next field to a stile and over this follow the field edge to a lane. Turn right to an imposing signpost indicating the way to Ashleworth Quay and walk down to the church and imposing tithe barn. The Boat Inn is a few yards further and a bridleway opposite follows the river bank towards Gloucester.

When the towpath was in commercial use it followed the eastern bank of the river from Gloucester. But the confluence with the River Chelt and the high cliff at Wainlode upstream necessitated the towpath changing banks. The Boat Inn provided refreshment for boatmen at the point where a chain ferry transferred the horses across the river.

The medieval Ashleworth Court and Tithe Barn, 40 yards long, are of limestone, whereas the Manor House is a timber framed building. The surrounding area is often flooded.

From the T junction turn right through the village passing the Queens Arms, and a road to the left. Continue around bends to a junction with Longridge Lane and follow this. Unfortunately *it is not along the ridge, where it would provide a splendid approach to the City, but along the foot of the slope. Although it is a pleasant and ancient way, views are restricted.*

Continue past Longridge Farm, through a gate into an open field, and follow the left hand boundary. From the next gateway fork diagonally right to the riverbank and follow it for half a mile. *Called the Long Reach, this straight length of river possibly relates to the days of sail, when Severn Trows, particularly going north, might have had a brief sail on the prevailing south westerly winds.* At a cross hedge and stream leave the river and follow the bridleway turning right up the hill to Home Farm. The alternative route from the Boat Inn continues along the riverbank to Maisemore.

Pass Maisemore Park, which is hidden from prying eyes by high hedges which also prevent an early glimpse of Gloucester, and continue to a junction and keep left. Maisemore Church on its hill comes into view on the right, and rounding a bend Gloucester cathedral appears against the background of Robinswood Hill and the Cotswold scarp.

> Who says 'Gloucester' sees a tall
> Fair fashioned shape of stone arise,
> That changes with the changing skies
> From joy to funereal gloom......
>
> The surprising, the enormous Severn Plain
> So wide, so fair
> From Crickley seen or Cooper's, my dear lane
> That holds all lane delightfulnesses there
> O Maisemore's darling way !
>
> *Ivor Gurney*

Ivor Gurney was born at Gloucester in 1890. A fellow chorister and student with Herbert Howells he was a great friend of another Gloucestershire poet Will Harvey of Minsterworth. Largely unrecognised during his short lifetime, his songs, based mainly on the work of English poets, are pastoral, reflective and melodious. He set few of his own poems to music but these portray local scenes in the pleasant countryside around Gloucester which he loved to ramble through. He is buried at Twigworth across the river where there is also a memorial to Herbert Howells.

Walk through Maisemore to the Gloucester-Ledbury road outside the White Hart Inn, where a celebratory drink to the Three Choirs Way might be in order?

Maes Mawr -a great field - may have referred to Alney Island (Olney Island to the Saxons and a place of formal meetings), which is enclosed by the two arms of the Severn and extends for more than two miles to the city.

Walk towards Gloucester and after crossing Maisemore bridge turn left on to a bridleway track. After about 300 yards turn right through a kissing gate and follow the field edge to a cross path and then left to the bank of the Severn's east channel. Continue along the river side path, passing under the city's orbital road, to a stile. Over this turn right to a footbridge and kissing gate and then left along a field boundary and under the railway viaduct where the outward section of the Three Choirs Way is rejoined.

Follow the track through trees to the footway alongside the road and follow it back to the river and, via the underpass and footbridge, to the cathedral at the end of, what I hope has been, an enjoyable circuit through the three counties.

* * *

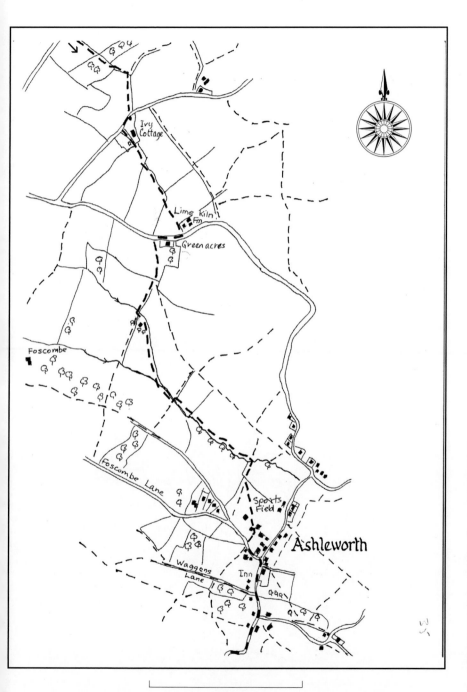

Half mile

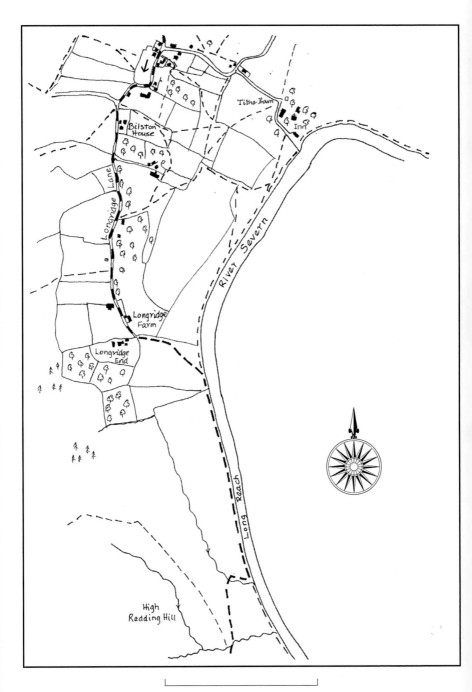

Half mile

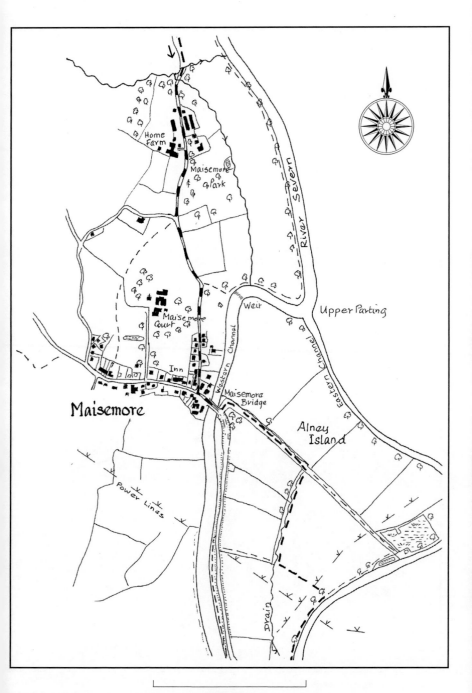

Maisemore

Home Farm

Maisemore Park

River Severn

Weir

Upper Parting

Maisemore Court

Eastern Channel

Western Channel

Inn

Maisemore Bridge

Alney Island

Power Lines

Drain

Half mile

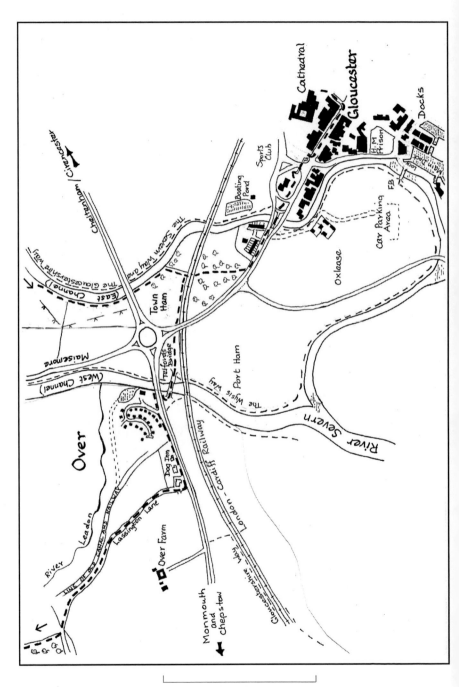

Half mile

Three Choirs Way Mileages

Gloucester			
Tibberton	6		
Cliffords Mesne	4.4	10.4	
Kilcot	2		
Marcle	5.2		
Sleaves Oak	3.2	10.4	20.8
Woolhope	2		
Haugh Wood	2.4		
Mordiford	1.2		
Hereford Cathedral	4.4	10.0	30.8
Lugwardine	3.2		
Withington	2.8		
Ocle Pychard	3.6	9.6	40.4
Much Cowarne	2		
Munderfield Row	5.6		
Stanford Bishop	2.4	10.0	50.4
Suckley Knowl	3.2		
Knightwick	2.8		
Broad Green	4	10.0	60.4
Broadheath	2.8		
Worcester Cathedral	3.2		
Carrington Bridge	2		
Stanbrook	2	10.0	70.4
Old Hills	1.5		
Madresfield	2		
Malvern Link Common	1.5		
Wyche Cutting	3.5		
British Camp	2.4	10.9	81.3
Hollybush	2.4		
Pendock	4.8		
Lowbands	1.2		
Staunton	2	10.4	91.7
Ashleworth	3.2		
Maisemore	3.2		
Gloucester Cathedral	2.4	8.8	100.5

THE GLOUCESTERSHIRE WAY

A continuous walk of 100 miles through the distinctive areas of the Forest of Dean, Severn Vale and Cotswold, taking a theme of 'Forest and Vale and High Blue Hill' from a poem, 'A Song of Gloucestershire' by F.W. Harvey.

THE WYSIS WAY

From the ancient earthwork of Offa's Dyke at Monmouth, built to the order of Offa, the powerful king of Mercia in 800 AD, to the infant Thames rising from the limestone high in Gloucestershire, The Wysis Way runs for 55 miles through the distinctive areas of the Forest of Dean, Severn Vale and Cotswold linking two great National Trails, Offa's Dyke Path and The Thames Path.

THE COTSWOLD CANALS WALK

The Stroudwater and Thames and Severn Canals traverse some of the most beautiful parts of the English countryside. For almost 50 miles from Framilode on the River Severn, to the Thames at Lechlade, the walk follows the line of these old canals, sometimes on the towpath past scenes redolent of industrial archaeology, elsewhere following field paths through pastoral countryside.

ST KENELM'S WAY

St Kenelm's Way is a walk of 60 miles through Worcestershire from the Clent Hills to the Cotswolds, tracing the legendary journey of the young prince's body from the site of his murder to his burial place at Winchcombe. The holy remains were carried ceremoniously by the monks of Winchcombe Abbey and wherever the cortege rested on the journey a crystal spring gushed forth.

Countryside Matters aims to produce descriptions of pleasant walking, through Gloucestershire and adjoining area, with a strong local connotation and a depth of feeling for the old footpath ways through the countryside.

All books available from the publisher at www.countryside-matters.co.uk